Consumer Guide To Digital Marketing

For Local Business Owners

Vera Ambuehl

© 2014 by **Vera Ambuehl**

All Rights Reserved. No part of this publication may be reproduced in any form or by any means, including scanning, photocopying, or otherwise without prior written permission of the copyright holder.

Cover Photo Credit, Pixabay.com

First Printing, 2014

ISBN Number: 1503115186

Printed in the United States of America

Disclaimer

This document contains an important overview of digital marketing for local business owners. The information is shared for the purpose of providing the reader with information they need in order to become a discerning consumer.

It is a <u>consumer guide</u>, not a "how-to" training guide. There should be no expectation that you will learn how to implement the many components of digital marketing from this short book.

Rather, this provides the "what" and "why" answers and explains the emergence of the industry made up of those who provide digital marketing services for local businesses.

Results of implementing these methods are not the same for everyone, and there is no stated guarantee of results for non-clients.

There are several factors and variables that come into play regarding any given business. One is implementation. Another is competence of the person or persons who perform the implementation. This author does not endorse or make specific recommendations of other providers who are unknown to her.

Results will also depend on the nature of the reader's product or business category, the conditions of the marketplace, as well as situations and elements that are beyond control.

As with any business endeavor, you assume all risk related to investment and money based on your own discretion and at your own expense.

Liability Disclaimer

You also assume all risks associated with using the following information. The reader is responsible for anything that may occur as a result of putting this information into action, regardless of interpretation.

The author cannot be held responsible in any way for the success or failure of any business as a result of the information presented in this book. It is your responsibility to conduct your own due diligence regarding the safe and successful operation of your business, whether or not you intend to apply any information received from this book.

Terms of Use

There are no resale rights or private label rights granted when purchasing this document.

Consumer Guide To Digital Marketing

For Local Business Owners

Dedication

This book is dedicated to ambitious, courageous entrepreneurs everywhere ... those who want and need to gain a better understanding of what digital marketing entails and why integrating cutting edge strategies can give them the advantage.

Thomas Paine wrote the following more than two hundred years ago, but it is still applicable.

The Entrepreneurs Credo

I do not choose to be a common man,
It is my right to be uncommon ... if I can.
I seek opportunity ... not security.
I do not wish to be a kept citizen.
Humbled and dulled by having the
State look after me.
I want to take the calculated risk;
To dream and to build.
To fail and to succeed.
I refuse to barter incentive for a dole;
I prefer the challenges of life
To the guaranteed existence;
The thrill of fulfillment
To the stale calm of Utopia.
I will not trade freedom for beneficence
Nor my dignity for a handout
I will never cower before any master

Nor bend to any threat.
It is my heritage to stand erect.
Proud and unafraid;
To think and to act for myself,
To enjoy the benefit of my creations
And to face the world boldly and say:
"This, with God's help, I have done
All this is what it means
To be an Entrepreneur."

~Thomas Paine

Contents

Section/Chapter Title	Page
Dedication	7
Introduction	11
Laggards Tax	17
SoMoLoCo	31
Social Marketing	43
Mobile Marketing	53
Local Marketing	73
Content Marketing	87
Authority Marketing	97
Lead Generation	111
Bionic Marketing	121
Conclusion	131
Resources	135
Terminology	141

Author Profile   149

Inspiring Quotes   151

Introduction

An article in a recent issue of the LIMA (Local Internet Marketing Association) Newsletter states, "Congratulations on becoming a Local Internet Marketer. Now nobody will understand what on earth you do for a living."

One of the things I'd like to share with you in this book is the existence of (and some details about) this relatively new industry . . . and how its members can help you.

If all the talk about "SEO","SEM", "clouds" that don't seem to indicate rain, and "cookies" that aren't edible frustrates you to the point of distraction, you will likely be relieved to learn . . . help is available.

This industry was **created to help you get more customers.** Yet, this may be the first time you've heard of it! It was created to fulfill the need local business owners currently have. Wherever you are in the world there's most likely a member of this industry nearby.

The fact is we're at a point of technical innovation spurred by consumer demand where local brick and mortar businesses are on the edge of a precipice - from which they will either evolve or devolve.

Blaming or 'waiting out' the economy, and 'hoping for the best' while avoiding the existence of this precipice will not serve them well.

I don't say this to be critical, I have deep admiration for entrepreneurs, and am one myself (though I didn't start out that way).

It's going to take the ingenuity, talents, creativity and dedicated efforts of each independent business owner to get our free market economic system back on track. Marketing is an essential part of the equation.

You'll learn my entrepreneurial story and how it revolves around technical innovations in a later chapter.

By the time you've made it through this book, you'll see the urgency in finding that fellow local business owner who will prove to be the key to bringing your business into the ongoing digital revolution.

This is where the majority of consumers have been for a while now . . . and where your business can flourish.

Your Local Internet Marketer is someone with the ability to transform your business from surviving to thriving, even in this challenging economic environment.

He or she can guide you as you adapt to technical innovations that provide multiple new opportunities to showcase your products and services – and to add products that will give you additional income.

Let the profits flow!

Note: *If you resist embracing new technologies, it's not your fault! In his book, <u>Pitch Anything</u>, author Oren Klaff says the part of our brain he refers to as our "Crocodile" brain is responsible. Research has determined this to be true.*

So, it's not your fault if you've fallen behind! Almost everyone resists change and we've definitely seen a lot of it in the area of technical innovation. We prefer to block it out because it's just one more major challenge facing us in our already hectic daily lives.

Unless you're an attorney, you know you need to consult one in order to deal with any business legal issues. Unless you're a C.P.A., you'll call one when you have an accounting or tax question. In fact, you probably have these professionals on speed dial already.

So, it follows that when it comes to the need for proper implementation of customer attraction (aka marketing strategy) in this digital era – most local small business owners need a hand from a friendly well trained professional.

The most important point to emphasize about achieving that desirable, but murkily defined "online presence" you keep hearing about is that creating it requires **both** an expertise in age old **marketing principles** and in the use of cutting edge technology tools to implement these marketing strategies.

Many local businesses count on their office staff to provide their marketing services, such as blog post writing, website updates, and social media posting. This is a huge savings if this employee has the marketing education, in addition to technical skills.

Cutting edge techniques are available for you to take advantage of today – but you won't hear about some of them or see them taught in college marketing courses yet. This means you can be ahead of the curve!

This book introduces you to an overview of "SoMoLoCo" (Social, Mobile, Local, and Content

Marketing – which I consider **the four pillars of Digital Marketing**) and the industry experts who are qualified to help provide services necessary to implement these value packed services.

Its goal is to provide you with the background that will turn you into an informed consumer, so you can get the help you need – with confidence.

Consider this your 'consumer report' of the local business marketing roadmap . . . enabling you to learn **what you're being advised to add to your marketing strategy, and why you need it.** I promise that's exactly what you will learn from this book!

Large corporations have a CMO (Chief Marketing Officer) to oversee the wide range of marketing initiatives taking place. Small, local businesses still have a growing number of Local Marketing Consultants to choose from, but the availability will dwindle as their need is widely recognized.

I sincerely hope you recognize that need and endeavor to find that other small business owner with the ability to help you. This will benefit your community, too, as you'll also be 'shopping local'.

Vera Ambuehl

Laggards Tax™

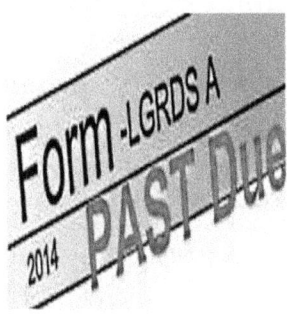

The widespread lack of adoption by the business community at large to innovative technologies has raised concerns about both security and business growth.

Achieving the growth, prosperity and resulting freedom that is possible today, especially for local brick and mortar businesses will require adoption of innovations widely embraced by consumers.

As you read the title of this chapter you're probably asking, "What in the world is "Laggards Tax™? Does such a tax really exist? Which state or federal form do I need?" Or, "I haven't paid that – how far behind am I by now?"

Please allow me to explain . . .

The term "Laggards" was used in a couple of news reports regarding the Target security breach where millions of customers were taken advantage of by cyber criminals. Several other large corporations lost a great deal of credibility stemming from that debacle, too.

The loss to consumers in peace-of-mind alone will never be fully calculated. Unfortunately, more of these horrific stories continue to be told.

In a YouTube video about the incident, the word "Laggards" was used to lament the lack of action from the business/financial community to upgrade to more secure technology. According to that video, technology has long been available that is impossible for hackers to infiltrate.

But the status quo was chosen, instead.

Also according to that video, credit cards with computer chips are available and should have replaced magnetic strip cards already, since those were developed in **1970**!

1970, hmm, amazing, isn't it? It struck me that the situation is very similar to usage of the technologies used in marketing businesses, both large and small. Consumers' stunningly fast evolving love affair with smartphones, especially, has made dramatic changes in our culture and behavior – far more than many people realize.

Consumers are now in the driver's seat – they're dictating change on the part of YOUR business!

There's no stronger or more compelling a catalyst for the adoption of these digital marketing strategies by businesses, because doing so means the difference between success and failure at some point down the road.

There is natural attrition throughout your current customer base, so being available to prospective customers on whatever media they use is essential.

Don't worry, the Laggards Tax™ problem is remarkably easy to fix!

Consumers search on their beloved smartphones, but **some (far too many) local businesses either cannot be found or have websites that are just too frustrating to navigate for the small screen user.** The majority of impatient mobile users just move on - to a competitor.

You've no doubt observed the dependence your customers have on their mobile devices. In fact, you, too, probably share that dependence in your own role as a consumer and "wearer of too many hats" business owner.

"Laggards Tax™", while not an official tax levied by any government entity is the loss of an **undetermined amount of money.** It's the result of delaying or avoiding implementation of marketing technologies that could be attracting many more customers and encouraging return visits and referrals by existing customers.

It's actually far more a loss than the taxes you pay that are collected by government entities – at least some of that money is spent on actual necessities!

You may be "leaving money on the table", but **you have no idea just how much money – or how big that table needs to be in order to hold it all!**

Even this present shaky (but recovering?) economy presents enormous opportunity.

Fortunately, unlike a 'real' tax imposed by the I.R.S., or local taxing authority, we can all;

 !!

The graphic on the previous page is not very attractive, but . . . the truth is it's no more unattractive than a future filled with that comfortable old standby, "business as usual".

How much is a customer worth to your business? For example, the lady who needs a haircut and searches for a hair salon (assume, for just a moment that's your business) on her smartphone, but doesn't find you! And, you're completely unaware of her existence, too.

You cannot know whether there's **any chance** she may have become a regular client purchasing hair color, manicures, pedicures, massages, and facials, in addition to monthly trims. In other words, she may have become one of your 'bread and butter' clients.

Years ago when I was an active participant in the hair salon industry that term was applied to weekly shampoo/set clients who routinely requested chemical services as needed (I think it still is used). They were "regulars", a reliable source of income.

These regulars were treated like gold in the successful high-end salons - and for good reason!

They provided referrals, and had family members who came **without** any advertising spend at all! That's pretty hard to beat, isn't it?

Are YOU missing out on goldmines like this?

Over the years I've seen study results published by companies like Forester, Nielsen, and Google. They point to consumer's consistently ignoring businesses because of a lack of a mobile website, missing listings in search, slow loading websites, and other inconveniences.

A speaker at an educational marketing event I attended last summer confided that he could be standing right in front of a restaurant, but if it didn't have a mobile presence, he'd ignore it . . . even though he was hungry!

And, what about restaurants? Maybe you own one. Can you see how potential revenue from customers who can't find you may be lowering your profits? Without the use of online metrics you have no idea how many people are searching for a specific type of restaurant, or which 'keywords' they're using to do so.

And before they pass through the door, are seated and place an order you won't know how hungry they are, whether they habitually add a glass of wine or bar drink to their tab, or even how many people make up that party.

If only you'd have been visible – you'd have met some of those prospective customers, who may have, by now, become loyal repeat customers.

Can you hear the "Cha-ching" of the cash register?

Because, if you were set up with online ordering, their table would be awaiting their arrival and your chefs and servers would be appropriately prepared to provide timely service. How many future loyal customers, referring their friends and family could your business handle?

You probably agree, your number of loyal customers multiplied by the lifetime value of each one would justify the <u>investment</u> in implementation of the latest technologies, systems and processes. Today, this is an investment, not an expense, because **results can be tracked and proven!**

Don't worry. This catastrophic plight that's crippling your ability to increase profits through steady growth no matter what the current state of the economy can quickly be remedied! Your Local Internet Marketer is equipped to provide the relevant solutions.

The Security Crisis - Affecting Local Businesses, Too

Speaking of the ominous danger of laggardly behavior, I feel I'd be doing you a disservice if I failed to share some security issues that are worrisome for local small businesses.

An article caught my attention awhile back. It was included in the May, 2014 issue of Business Solutions, a magazine that is mailed out to members of the IT industry. As a long-time member of that industry, my husband receives several related magazines.

This article was authored by Mr. Jay McCall and cites results of a survey of more than 1000 SMB's (Small/Medium Businesses). The survey was conducted by MacAfee, in conjunction with Office Depot.

One point cited states that <u>only half</u> of the small business respondents said they used any <u>internet security</u> at all! Does that strike you as scary?

I'm guessing that is does, as it's such an important issue. Even if you don't store client identification numbers, having your entire customer list or your own financial or marketing data stolen or experiencing productivity sapping viruses or malicious attacks can cripple a business.

The entire article is available online. The title is "**Why Small Business Security Is Such a Big Deal**". If you're interested in reading it you should be able to locate it by searching that title and the author's name using your desktop computer. I couldn't locate a mobile version of it.

Cyber security is a topic of special interest especially to any business owner allowing employees to bring their own devices (BYOD) to access company data. Even without this the importance of security measures cannot be minimized.

Avoiding the adoption of a security protection plan will no doubt become a financial disaster for small businesses if they ignore the issue.

Recent issues of VAR (Value Added Reseller) Magazine are lamenting the lack of adoption to current technologies they deem necessary, too. One chief concern is with POS (Point of Sale) and the need to upgrade to more secure means of transaction processing that safeguards customer credit card information.

Small local businesses are just as vulnerable as big business (like Target and others) and a data breach that negatively affects your clients could be disastrous to the goodwill you've worked so hard to build.

You probably don't want to spend hard earned resources to address the PR disaster alone, or be forced into an emergency wide-scale IT overhaul. Prevention is probably the safest policy.

Just like in marketing, the 'Mobile Revolution' has had a massive effect on business systems and processes. Solutions are available to you in this regard, as well. Upgrading could save you some very real headaches in the near future.

Cyber Security is not a topic I've studied much and I definitely don't feel qualified on this level of technology. I am deeply concerned about its effect on local businesses, though.

I recently heard a gentleman being interviewed on the radio who is an expert on the topic. His name is Brian Krebs, and he's researched this issue extensively. He recently published a book entitled, **Spam Nation:** The Inside Story of Organized Cyber Crime – From Global Epidemic to Your Front Door.

Mr. Krebs is the Founder of the award winning Blog, www.krebsonsecurity.com, and a former reporter at the Washington Post. His book is available on Amazon.com. He's done investigations of the cybercrime activities in Russia and around the world.

I haven't read his book yet, but am looking forward to learning about his investigation. We all need to be armed with education like this, though it is rather frightening! I had planned to add this book to the Resources chapter, but I really want to make you aware of it while you're reading this section.

A Solution Emerges for POS, Security and

MORE . . .

This came to my attention unexpectedly! In 2012, I contacted First Data Corporation which for more than forty years has been a global leader in merchant services solutions and security.

I had read about their participation in NFC (Near Field Communications) and security in the development of Google Wallet. I wanted to have a mobile payment solution to offer local business owners.

They invited me to participate in their Referral Partner program. But, I found no business owners at the time who were interested.

It seems everything I've learned has taken several years to become mainstream and hasn't totally reached that point in my area yet.

That's probably why a long-time web developer asked if I had "made all this up" at a trade show a couple of years ago. When people hear about them for the first time, many recent innovations sound like a complete fantasy! Be ready for even more "futuristic" concepts coming soon, though.

Anyway, a few months ago I had my website re-done and until the other day had neglected to add First Data's information to it.

Fast forward to just a few days ago - I received a phone call from a First Data representative. I had just been thinking about them and was pleased to be in touch again.

They sent me an email with a few links to their latest products and I was truly blown away!

It turns out, they have contributed largely to the infrastructure of Apple's Pay, too (tap to pay with your smartphone). A recent article in the Wall Street Journal online cited them for their contribution and leadership in that technology.

Speaking of cybercrime, one of the important solutions they currently offer has to do with preventing hackers from getting your customer's credit card numbers!

They provide "Tokenization", which replaces the credit card number with one that is irrelevant and useless to the hacker. And, they use "Encryption", which transforms plain text information into a non-readable form called "ciphertext".

On their website, (www.firstdata.com) they explain that this protects against customer credit card numbers being visible to hackers at the two most vulnerable times during a transaction.

Combined with their new "Clover Station", a sleek modern looking desktop hardware system made for small businesses, they're providing everything necessary to keep your business up-and-running <u>and secure</u>.

The Clover Station does everything from inventory tracking, employee management, customer insight for CRM (Customer Relationship Management) and, of course, payment processing.

The Clover also integrates with Apple's Pay Station <u>and</u> with Perka's Loyalty Coupons!

The Perka integration is very exciting, to me, anyway. I called them a few years ago and was very impressed with their loyalty system – glad to hear they've grown!

Mobile coupons have been available for several years. They should have completely replaced paper by now, as consumers seem to love them (they never forget to bring them, because they <u>never leave home without their smartphone</u>).

Starbucks has been one of the pioneers in the use of mobile loyalty and other mobile initiatives. But, these programs are great in helping every business grow! **Yours, included!**

Well, I won't go on and on, but if you have been considering an update in your transaction processing, or just want to be up-to-date on what's available, it's worth the time to see what's over at www.firstdata.com. They offer a wide variety of solutions that will ease your security concerns.

Do your own research and learn as much as possible about this topic from multiple sources so you can be confident no matter what decisions you make.

SoMoLoCo

Someone in the industry began using "SoMoLoCo" as a shortcut to denote Social, Mobile, Local, and Content Marketing a couple of years ago – I first saw it used on one of the major technology blogs. I like it.

It adequately describes much of what we Local Internet Marketers do to help business owners like you. It's unclear who to credit for the 'invention' of this acronym, though, or I would do so.

Below, you can see some of the more important elements of each of the four pillars and how they integrate with each other.

Lead Generation is a traditionally well-known and exceedingly important business function and there's a separate chapter on it with examples on how it can be used in today's digital marketing, as a function of Direct Response Marketing.

I've made every effort to spell out acronyms and explain other terminology, but if you still have questions, I've provided an email address so you can ask. I'll personally answer each one.

By the time you finish reading this book I believe you'll be prepared to carry on a productive conversation with the most learned of internet marketers and local marketing consultants.

This will help you make an informed selection. Your Local Internet Marketer will appreciate your ability to discuss these topics, too.

How do you choose the right Local Internet Marketer to help you?

I would say a red flag would be someone who claims to be <u>an expert in everything</u>!

That's not to say, there aren't people much brighter than I am who somehow manage to handle the entire mountain of work with precision excellence (kudo's to them). But, there are so many skills to learn and it's difficult to have great expertise in every single one.

This industry could be compared to the medical profession, in that people do often specialize in only one or two elements of digital marketing.

The big difference is that before deciding on a specialty, a medical student is <u>required</u> to learn and understand how every system of human anatomy works and how the systems work together - before choosing their specialty.

That doesn't necessarily happen in marketing, and this probably accounts for some of the general skepticism and distrust that appears to exist around the very word, "marketing". I suspect it also contributes to business owners confusion, overwhelm and hesitation to get started acquiring digital assets.

In the medical profession, though human anatomy hasn't changed . . . the approaches to healing have. In marketing, the principles haven't changed, but new tools and techniques used to implement them change very frequently.

Many people in this industry call their business an "Agency". That's good, because it means they delegate the services they don't personally specialize in to people with a high level of expertise in specific skill sets.

This gives them the capability to offer the full range of digital services needed by their local business community.

I do that, as well, because I've discovered it's more practical to spend my time meeting and getting to know clients so I can accurately represent them in promotions and other content needs that I specialize in.

My vision is to maintain long-term relationships with clients through demonstrating value, competence and the desire, ability and willingness to serve them. I believe most members of this industry share those goals.

There are a growing number of global companies entering into this industry, as well, in order to fulfill the apparent need.

Yellow Page directories are all building their digital platforms where they now specialize in local online advertising and digital services, as need for traditional phone directories continually decreases.

Your decision about where to access the help you need will depend partly upon how much you value personalized service and unique-to-you hands-on approaches.

My view is that cookie cutter approaches are wasteful, especially in the realm of content creation. Today, if you advertise just like everyone else in your industry you tend to be ignored.

You and your business are very unique and it's that uniqueness that attracts and encourages loyalty from your customers. The Internet is crowded with choices and you need to stand out (by being the authentic YOU) so you can attract new customers, too.

The basics, like SEO, are far less restrictive in that regard. They actually can be done adequately from any place with internet access. The initial step in analyzing a business' online presence is usually done entirely through the use of software.

It's quite accurate, but requires a follow-up look by human eyes in order to ensure a maximum advantage for each business.

Global local business marketing companies hire a local representative in most localities to get to know business owners and to act as sales representatives. They know that people prefer to buy from other people, rather than a faceless global corporation . . . it's an issue of trust and connection.

Representatives of global companies may change often compared to a locally owned company, and will have less autonomy, but an arrangement like this may suit you fine.

What is more important is your being prepared with a basic knowledge of what you need, so you can keep your costs down while still receiving the quality services you deserve.

As an agency owner, I've recently added a team of technical experts. Each person on the team specializes in what he or she does best. Many agencies are made up of joint partnerships, each available to contribute where client needs exist.

Since I don't think it's fair to ask potential clients to do what I won't, I've also engaged my technical team to provide SEO services for my own company. Had I not done so, I wouldn't have had time to write this book.

How "Practicing What I Preach" Is Helping Me Understand the Viewpoint of the Local Business Owner

Products and services need to be displayed so that prospective clients can gauge their quality and effectiveness. My growing online presence (currently in the very early stages) serves as a 'display model' of my team's work, though they have served thousands of other businesses, too.

A major copywriting mandate is to "know your target client" and, in fact, to create a profile (or avatar) of one's ideal client - <u>even before</u> touching the keyboard!

From the standpoint of understanding what it's like to invest in digital marketing services, I can definitely identify with my chosen client avatar.
My technical team is engaged in demonstrating their work on my online presence and I'm paying them to do so. And, you know what? It hurts to pay out that money every month!

Yet, at the same time I understand and firmly believe in the need for and effectiveness of digital marketing to result in growth— facts show it's not a nebulous question of the 'chicken or the egg'.

And, historically, so many businesses that began or continued to do marketing during slow economic times, such as the Great Depression and a number of recessions since have flourished.

Many who halted marketing campaigns to 'wait out' a recession no longer existed by the time economic conditions had improved. You've probably read or watched documentaries that relate the history and progress of businesses like Proctor and Gamble, and other long-time 'household name' businesses.

It is normal for online services to be charged for in advance of their completion and the reason is once they're completed they cannot be taken back – they're in your possession, whether you follow through with your payment or not.

And as you'll learn in a later chapter, digital marketing services are an on-going long-term need, rather than a one-time task.

To be on the safe side, you may want to select a local marketing service provider with apparent evidence of having marketed his or her own business. That really is the most basic evidence of what they are able to provide for you.

For years, local businesses simply invested in Yellow Page listings every year, but now digital has largely taken precedence. At this point in history, other than doing all the necessary work yourself . . . the primary decision is selecting the best available service provider to bring your business into the digital age.

Make the Choice That Best Suits You

Once you've identified a couple of good choices, the one you choose will likely be determined by whether you like working with the representative of that company.

That's usually how it works. People buy from other people, based upon whether they like them and trust them – and they need to get to know them first.

I'm confident that you'll find a Local Internet Marketer you like, wherever you are in the world.

In order to find someone in an online search, keywords such as "online advertising agency", "marketing consultant", or "small business development" will help you, in addition to "local or offline marketing".

There's a glossary of terms later in this book to get more ideas if you need to.

Though technology allows us to do this work from anywhere, I prefer to serve businesses that are within a reasonable distance from me. I firmly believe marketing can have a huge influence in growing the economy and I'd love to serve my own area and see many of the empty buildings fill up with brand new entrepreneurial activities.

Local Internet Marketing was intended to be done 'locally' at the time I learned about it in 2009. Then, specific high-value-per-client industries began being targeted nationally, even globally . . . today, lower revenue per client businesses are often ignored.

This is unfortunate, as every single business can benefit from today's digital marketing strategies. Besides, every business usually starts out small; it makes sense to provide these services to them so they can grow faster and larger.

A marketing budget is a necessity today regardless of the type of business or its size. Many savvy business owners already understand this.

Anyway, as long as local business owners prove to be as loyal to my business as I am to theirs, I'll love serving my own community and the surrounding region. Serving locally means I can spend a little time in a business' physical space and that helps me market a business more authentically.

It's very helpful to observe the clientele, and just take in the atmosphere, developing insight while remaining in the background like an impartial 'invisible' observer.

Not to brag, but I seem to be one of the best when it comes to having the innate ability to blend into the woodwork! ☺ After multiple attempts to change my own nature and personality, I eventually figured out it just wasn't going to happen.

That being the case, I had to identify the elusive and well-hidden strength in being "too quiet". At some point I recognized that it translates into being observant, insightful, and an expert at listening.

My technical team communicates with clients by email about the tasks they're involved in. But, I feel it's necessary to meet a potential client in person, at least once before deciding whether they will be a good fit for my company. Those who feel the same way may appreciate this, as they want to be able to judge whether I'm a good fit for them, too.

A visit to client businesses also provides an opportunity to speak with happy customers who may consent to shooting a quick video testimonial! These are very powerful and perceived as more 'truthful and real' than traditional text testimonials.

Make Your Choice of a Marketer Based Upon Plenty of Research

You probably already do your due diligence when it comes to investing your money – you wouldn't still have a business if you didn't.

Search all the alternatives near you. Check out the websites (if they don't have an online presence, you may agree that they should take care of that task before 'hanging out their shingle'). When you feel you've found a good fit, ask to meet with the owner or local representative.

You'll know when you've made the right choice, then **you'll have found one of the best partners possible . . . someone who cares**

as much about your business succeeding as you do!

***

Everywhere, it seems, <u>Social Media</u> has captured most of the attention, but, it's <u>not the only important element to digital marketing</u>.

Everything works together. What's most important? "All of the above", to some degree - based upon the specifics of your business.

It's like baking a pumpkin pie only to realize later you forgot to add any sugar. I have it on good authority that doing so will make your meal memorable . . . but, not in a good way.

Social Media will be the topic of the next chapter.

Social Media

As you know, social media marketing has been popular for several years and it plays a huge and very important role in the marketing of all businesses and organizations. Many local businesses have gotten on the bandwagon in just the past three years. Kudos to them! And, to you if you're one of them!

Getting the work done

Where to find the time is the question often in the forefront for business owners. The decision of whether to outsource the work, delegate the task to a family member or employee, or do it yourself is difficult.

Professional Social Media Managers can do all the work for you while it appears that you are actually the one laboring over clever, friendly, educational, entertaining and engaging posts!

It can be the best of both worlds to have someone attuned to your business with the ability to write in your voice who has a sense of when you should be consulted to step in; and is familiar with your community.

The benefits of hiring a **local** Social Media Manager include their ability to:

> - Interact knowledgably and comfortably about area events
> - Talk about local sports, school teams, colors and mascots
> - Interact on 'ice-breaker' topics like weather conditions
> - Comment on local and business news
> - Understand local historic landmarks and their significance
> - Know your business, your employees, and your customers

You need for that person to be able to effectively 'clone' you. I've been a ghostwriter for quite some time and for me it's best to have the opportunity to spend some time with my 'author' in person in order to pick up on their personality and speech patterns.

By phone I miss out on much of the body language and interaction with others that I can witness in person, though follow-up can certainly be done remotely.

This is especially true for a very small business where the owner is actively involved and 'present' in the business every day. If customers interact with you every day they'll recognize 'out of character' comments on social media, and that will diminish your credibility and customer participation. It's important, in my opinion, for the owner of a small local business to be the face of that business.

In larger businesses often someone in administration will be the social media contact person. He or she may not face customers daily, so as long as the conversations are kept in a personable and professional tone a social media manager may not need to be as closely attuned.

Communication can be through Skype, Google Hangouts, or a conference call system. It obviously works quite adequately for many medium and large businesses.

It's well worth ensuring that your social media manager has the necessary background in creating varied and relevant content, not just the ability to handle the technical aspects.

Otherwise well intentioned people may tend to come across as pushy or overly "salesy" (as in "Hey, buy our Stuff!" 24 x 7), simply because that's what they think is expected.

Once they learn the importance of giving value, being engaging, and providing relevant, interesting content and using marketing principles, they'll likely handle the job admirably. One fundamental acronym knowledgeable marketing professionals are familiar with is AIDA.

AIDA stands for **A**wareness, **I**nterest, **D**esire, and **A**ction. Not being aware of marketing basics such as this and many others can be a serious obstacle to attracting and retaining customers (aka business growth).

You'll want to feel assured that your social media participation is in tune with the values and mission of your business. These are the all-important foundations upon which a business is built; they don't warrant altering or ignoring.

Without needing to constantly spend your valuable time checking on your social media you'll want to feel confident it's being handled to your satisfaction.

There are numerous modestly priced social media courses online, as well as in local community colleges where an employee or family member could receive training.

Kate Buck, Jr. recently announced the launch of a new course. I'm sure you could check it out by 'Googling' her name. She's very skilled in all social media platforms. I took her earlier course, "Let's get Social", heard her present and met her at a marketing event in San Antonio in 2011 - she's one of the best - obviously passionate and well informed about all the Social Media platforms!

You'll no doubt find recommendations from friends and relatives, too. You'll want to ensure that your business, no doubt one of your most valuable assets, is represented by a person with professional skills on all the relevant platforms you choose to join.

As the SoMoLoCo chart shown earlier indicates, Social Media integrates with Local, Mobile, and Content, the other three leading 'pillars' of 21st Century digital marketing.

More and more people access their favorite social media platforms through a mobile app in direct proportion to the growth in adoption of mobile devices.

Since Google has so much to do with being found, it's a necessity, but in a local search context is a function of Local Marketing, which is addressed in the chapter by that name. Though, it does have the social Google + layered into it.

It's not just the social platforms you think of first that are in the 'social' category; You Tube (Video Marketing is HUGE – very important for small businesses!), your blog (comments), forums, and other platforms are social in nature, as well. Amazon.com is social with its reviews feature, and continuing new means of interacting.

Online Reputation

Social 'proof' is everywhere and, of course, you can't believe everything you read. It has been said that this is 'the era of the customer', because of the ability for them to write reviews on so many online platforms.

News, <u>especially bad news</u> spreads quickly, as I'm sure you've experienced! That's why it's so important to monitor and be proactive about the reputation of your business. Many people take great stock in what they see online. Shockingly, many believe it's 100% true!

Recent studies reveal that online reviews garner almost as much trust in the minds of consumers as personal recommendations. This means having one or more devastating reviews visible for even a few days can relegate you to the "Laggards Tax™" situation.

You'll have no idea who or how many prospective customers have decided to 'take a pass' on even checking out your website after seeing negative reviews!

Legendary Direct Marketer, Dan Kennedy, once emphasized (and continues to promote) the importance and our responsibility to be pro-active about monitoring, even taking measures to ensure that positive information about us gets published.

One of his most often quoted statements is, "The simple truth is, if you aren't deliberately, systematically, methodically – or rapidly and dramatically **establishing yourself as a celebrity, at least to your clientele and target market**, you're asleep at the wheel, ignoring what is fueling the entire economy around you, neglecting development of a measurably valuable asset."

After all, undoing a bad reputation online takes time, money and skill, and it's not an overnight process. If you've already followed Mr. Kennedy's counsel, you won't be hurt as badly.

This is certainly not to advise anyone to lie! That's not being authentic – or honest. But, if you've been in business for a few years you surely have had a few "wins" or newsworthy events. They need to be published – this helps protect your livelihood – an important asset that affects other's lives, too!

Even if you don't have that many highlights, people would appreciate learning a bit about you before picking up the phone to make an appointment.

Your online reputation can be built up over time as you publish Press Releases, write articles and submit them as a guest blogger or submit them to print magazines – and, write a book or two!

You'll learn about more opportunities in the Content and Authority Marketing chapters.

Reviews Acquisition and Management

Regular attention and proactive strategies to encourage your happy customers to provide reviews will save a lot of heartache.

Caution – they should never be faked or paid for, though!

Most Local Online Marketers provide Reputation Management as a service. You can select a system that encourages feedback from your most loyal customers by making the process fast and convenient, too, which also encourages referrals. New methods of acquiring reviews pop up frequently.

One often-used solution is to funnel positive reviews to one of the online review sites, such as your Google Plus Local Page while diverting negative reviews to your business email address.

This allows you to resolve those rare customer dissatisfaction issues quietly without them being addressed in front of a world-wide audience via the social web.

There is so much information available on the topic of social media it leads many business owners to believe it is the only type of marketing they should concern themselves with beyond having a website . . . you're smart to be reading this because you'll soon understand how off-the-mark that 'myth' is.

The next chapter will cover mobile marketing; I think you'll find it very interesting. Some business owners I've spoken with were under the impression it was all about a car with a sign on it . . . driving around advertising a business. That certainly happens, too, so it makes sense in a way, right?

Mobile Marketing

Have You Taken Your Business Mobile Yet?

If not, the goal to do so <u>should rank very highly</u> on your to-do list. Most Local Internet Marketers either provide mobile websites and mobile marketing services or have a working relationship with someone else who does it for their clients.

Mobility, ensuring your business information is easily found and readable on a small smartphone screen is of paramount importance.

The fact that 'everyone' uses a mobile device is widely apparent no matter where you go. No doubt you're an enthusiastic user of this exciting and convenient technology, too. The freedom of the 'unplugged' lifestyle is so liberating!

Your business now desperately needs a mobile presence, if one is not yet in place.

Customers simply expect the businesses they deal with to stay up-to-date and provide simplicity and convenience. They tend to have **ZERO empathy** for those who don't.

Studies point to the tendency for mobile users to be impatient, to want what they want . . . when they want it.

So, what all do you need to bring your business current?

- Definitely, a **mobile website** that features a click-to-call, map and directions, your office hours, and a link to your full site - at a bare minimum.
- A services, product, or menu page is very helpful.
- Punch-card loyalty systems are very popular with consumers and a great substitute for plastic cards or paper they habitually lose or forget to bring with them.
- Consumers really appreciate **mobile coupons**. Paper coupons are a hassle and are so easily forgotten, not to mention – passé.
- A **lead generation** page is a no-brainer! Many local businesses don't have one on their website yet, but in the Internet Marketing world lead generation is paramount.
- If you work on an appointment basis you (and your clients/patients) may wish to opt in for **SMS** (Simple Message System, a.k.a. text message) **appointment reminders**. Many households are giving up their landline phones, as every member of the family has a smartphone or other mobile device. This allows for almost instant confirmations or re-scheduling.

"No-shows" are so expensive! (You can't get that time back!). Alternatively, these can also be done through "Push Notifications" if you have an app.

- Once you've collected contact information using your means of lead generation, you'll want to stay in contact with each of these customers. It is this contact through a mobile device that makes up the communication referred to as "**Mobile Marketing**".

- Integrating a **QR Code** into your mobile strategy can be done in several ways, using a combination of in-store signage, online notification, and direct mail to invite your customers' participation.

- Lest we forget, how would you like to be able to invite your customers to "Download our **Mobile App**"? Sounds cool, doesn't it? It is, and it's a great convenience for your customers! You don't even need to have a full blown app on one of the app stores in order to be able to make that offer! Ask about getting your own "web app", then promote it in-store, your customers will appreciate the convenience!

- The one alternative to a separate mobile website is a responsive website that fits whichever size screen the user has. This means it serves your customers whether they're using a desktop, tablet or mobile device.

Personally, I love the looks and extra functions available in mobile websites, and those that contain 'just the basics' are usually fast loading and very convenient for consumers. When they include a home screen app clients can download they are especially consumer-friendly!

How can consumers forget you when they see that app every time they look at their home screen?

It's like 24 x 7 advertising! Easily shareable, too. And, it's so simple for them to call you when they have just a minute to arrange an appointment. Software code on your desktop website can detect the device a user is on and redirect them to the mobile version.

Or, you can advertise the app on your website, in-store and in all your other marketing. Customers can download your app and access it within seconds. You can use a QR Code that directs to it.

Don't overlook getting your business app on the app stores, either! Costs have come down since the first apps were developed, often they're now in the $1200 - $3000 range for small businesses. For larger organizations they're often used internally for communications.

More and more features are being added to the range of possibilities in mobile marketing, some are still "ideas in progress", but most are really amazing.

Smartphone usage has grown to the point now that there are <u>more searches done on mobile devices than on desktop computers</u>. Many are local searches!

BYOD (Bring Your Own Device) has melded the interests of IT (Information Technology), Marketing, and Internet Security.

POS (Point of Sale) is going through multiple transitions due to the need for mobile commerce solutions. Cash register add-on devices are available for scanning a smartphone screen (as in processing mobile coupons).

In fact, Point of Sale (POS), because of smartphone and other mobile device use is a very important and rapidly evolving business right now.

Virtual currency (crypto currency), such as **Bitcoin** will no doubt play a growing role in local e-commerce, especially on mobile, as it is now used in many large enterprises. More than 600,000 businesses worldwide (many online) accept it for payment, according to recent reports.

ATM type machines that exchange Bitcoin for other currencies are increasing in number and the growth in acceptance is apparent. According to a recent news report, the City of San Francisco is either in the process of having one installed or has just completed the project.

They'll likely become very common everywhere.

Due to the recent Mt. Gox scandal (you probably heard about it on the news) the price and popularity declined for a while. Bitcoin appears to have a bright future, even so.

Soon, your customers may begin asking whether you accept Bitcoin.

Many people already invest in this currency or "mine" it. It has no physical mass, but exists on a "virtual wallet". There are other "crypto currencies", as well and they can be traded as an investment or used in commerce, too. Bitcoin is seen as the 'safest' and most legitimate.

Mobile has been declared the 7th **Mass Media** – meaning it reaches at least 95% of the people in the world! The printing press was number one, and the Internet was number six.

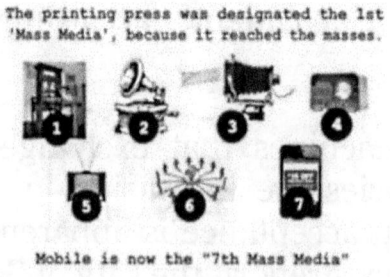

Mobile is now the "7th Mass Media"

Five Current Mobile Statistics:

- At least 50% of local searches are now conducted via a mobile device. This stat increases frequently.

- The Open Rate for text messages is above 90%, within five minutes (but don't say 'goodbye' to email yet – you probably open your email on mobile, as many of your customers do).

- Mobile barcodes (such as QR Codes) are 'an unprecedented marketing vehicle'. As mentioned, they are a much needed and currently under-used bridge between online and offline content.

- Mobile provides computerized analytics proving the effectiveness of your mobile marketing effort, and making unlimited testing possible.

- Geo-fencing and other **Location Based Marketing** methods are evolving and spreading to include an almost endless list of applications. Those applications include:
    - Location Discovery
    - Location Based Advertising
    - Friend Finder

o Shopping/Networking

Clearly, we are living in a 'Big Wide Wonderful Mobile World'

Not sure whether your business website is mobile compatible?

Ask Google:
https://www.google.com/webmasters/tools/mobile-friendly/

Invitation to Join a Mobile Campaign:

Combining a coupon with an invitation to a mobile campaign is one method of letting your customers know you've 'gone mobile'. These can be in the form of in-store signage, an ad or flyer, or advertisement on a different platform.

The word "pizza" in this mobile campaign invitation example is known as the "keyword" and the numbers are called the "short code". Keywords need to be unique, that is, you may be denied the single keyword you request if it is already being used by another subscriber to the mobile marketing platform you're using.

You can use two words together, such as "bestpizza". That's not a typo. The words need to be together in order for the software to recognize the keyword.

Each mobile marketing platform has a unique "short code". Short codes used to be 'dedicated', but 'shared' codes are now available, meaning prices are reasonable for all business sizes.

Most businesses run many keyword campaigns representing the variety of products they offer, but feel free to start with just one so you can gauge customer response. I think you'll be pleasantly surprised!

The text at the bottom (Stop, Help, Rates, Frequency of messages to expect) is required by rules, regulations, and best practices created by the global Mobile Marketing Association and the CTIA (Cellular Telecommunications Industry Association).

Similar regulations have since been passed through the FCC (Federal Communications Commission) and FTC (Federal Trade Commission). <u>These are strictly enforced</u>.

The Legal Requirements Deserve a Detailed Explanation:

- "**STOP** to End", or "**STOP** to Stop" lets the receiver know that they are free to reply with the message "STOP" in order to get their cell number deleted from that specific list – the equivalent to the "unsubscribe" option you should find at the bottom of any commercial email.
- "**HELP** For Help" lets the consumer know they can enter that word for support or for a link to Privacy Policies/Terms of Service (TOS). Always provide these, or a link to where they are published.
- "Message and Data Rates Apply", normally abbreviated, reminds the receiver that whatever texting plan they've chosen through their carrier

will apply as a member of that list. In other words, they may be billed.
- You must tell the consumer how many messages they can expect to receive each month (the recommended number is between two and four).

There is a character limit, but if needed two separate messages can be used. Whenever a message is sent, it should begin with your business name so the receiver knows who it's coming from.

As when you normally begin a telephone conversation by stating who you are and the company you are calling from, this should also be clear to recipients of text messages.

Regulations are a very important issue, as huge penalties were imposed by the government after laws were put in place in October, 2013. These laws are all about the rights of consumers to avoid receiving messages or emails they haven't agreed to receive. Think "**No Spam**", period.

Every customer must indicate their approval to receive messages from you – especially emails or text messages - in writing, and you need to keep proof of that approval.

Don't worry too much, though, as the appropriate email or mobile marketing platforms also have systems in place that include compliance.

As long as you don't add names/numbers to your list of people who haven't gone through the system and provided their approval to receive your messages, you'll most likely be abiding by the regulations when using a high quality provider. Each has contact information or a helpdesk you can use if you have questions.

If unwanted text messages were a problem for you, you've probably noticed a sudden and remarkable reduction in them lately, as offenders were dealt with severely (up to $16,000 per incidence penalties, <u>per individual</u>!).

Basically, cell phone numbers were added to federal Do-Not-Call regulations previously only pertaining to landline phone numbers. Non-compliance is now unmanageably expensive!

QR Code Marketing

You're no doubt aware of QR Codes, mentioned (and used) earlier. They've been around several years. They're a great mobile tool! They serve as a bridge; connecting the virtual online and physical realities.

If you're accustomed to sending postcards or other direct mail pieces and those convert well for you, you may want to update them by adding either a mobile campaign invitation or a QR code that links to mobile content your customers may appreciate, such as a mobile coupon.

During this seemingly never-ending era of transitioning from paper, to digital some Yellow Page publishers are using QR Codes in their ads, though I don't know whether it's increasing the desired results. In my area, phone books are often left below mail boxes until someone picks them up for recycling.

For decades we've heard the paperless office being promoted and predicted, but it is taking a very long time for our society to feel comfortable without physical records.

Like newspapers, yellow page providers are moving to online platforms, though, as are most facets of our culture.

There is still room for many old school marketing practices, especially when they're updated with digital aspects. Direct Mail, done right, is often effective, especially when used as a direct response media. People get far less of it these days so they tend to pay more attention to it.

Though QR Codes are being used with much greater frequency, I believe they're still far under-used by small local businesses simply because we are in a stage of transition. Local consumers for the most part definitely appear to know what how to scan QR Codes, so don't be afraid to get started with them.

Dynamic QR Codes

QR Codes can be dynamic, as well as static.

"Dynamic" means they can be programmed to change in results either by the minute, the hour, day week or month (whichever you choose). It's a very convenient way to keep customers updated about your events, daily or weekly specials, meetings, and more.

For example, some daycare facilities use dynamic QR Codes to keep parents updated on the planned daily lunch menu, so they can make alternative plans if they want their child to eat something different because of an allergy or other reason. Often, the facility will have the dynamic QR Codes printed on a refrigerator magnet.

It saves them paper clutter, and expense – the parents put the magnet on their refrigerator, where it's quick and easy to scan as they pass by during their morning scramble . . . without a frantic search for that elusive piece of paper.

Some clubs, churches, little leagues, and businesses hand out (or sell as a fundraising campaign) items like refrigerator magnets with a dynamic QR Code printed on it so their customers/members can stay on top of schedules anytime.

Obviously, this saves both work and paper, since the updates only need to be added once online. Having the magnets printed professionally will add to their perceived value.

QR Codes are 2 dimensional barcodes and they were actually invented in the 1990's by a subsidiary of Toyota (Denso Corporation) for the purpose of scanning automobile parts more quickly than could be done with one dimensional barcodes. Usually, you'll see QR codes in black.

You can have them created in any color now, but they must have a strong contrast to the background. Many QR Code creation platforms allow multi-color and accept the embedding of a logo or another image choice.

The QR Code shown here directs to a video on YouTube. It's by Marie Forleo who is interviewing Brendon Burchard about his book **The Charge**. This is a fairly random selection on my part, but I have read Brendon Burchard's book; it's very motivating. Go ahead – if this is still new to you, scan the code. Take a few minutes to watch the video, too – very enlightening.

This code was generated using the code generator at QRStuff. There are a number of QR Code generators online. Just do a Google search for them if you want to use a code like this. <u>Never direct to a web page that is not properly sized for smartphones, though</u>.

QR Codes are great for businesses such as real estate, as they can be put on signs directing to a virtual tour (a slider or video) of the rooms inside a home.

If you have a lot of characters in your URL (website address) QR Stuff and other generators have built in URL 'shorteners'.

Using the shortener makes the code less cluttered looking, and faster to read. You can always shorten the url before entering it into the generator, too, using Google's shortener or one of the other alternatives, such as bit.ly.

If a code cannot be read after being printed, the problem may be too low a printer resolution, rather than an issue with your QR Code Reader or creator.

Always test before adding a QR Code to any marketing material and always direct them to mobile content **only**, rather than your desk-top website. I know, I'm repeating that, but it is very important.

NFC Tags/Stickers

You'll no doubt see more Near Field Communications (NFC) being used, too. In marketing, as well as other industries they also are used to bridge the gap between the physical and the virtual world.

They're used currently on Android phone systems, though the latest iphone is predicted to be compatible with NFC, too. They do include Tap to Pay for credit card payments.

Other than for marketing, they've been used for several years. Google's Wallet came out a few years ago. Walmart and other retail stores have been using NFC for a couple of years for inventory tracking.

It saves a great deal of time (which translates into payroll dollars) to use an NFC Reader to count a stack of shirts or jeans, rather than manually counting one at a time. It can also tell the employee inventory details on the number of items held in the store's "back room".

So, even if you don't think you've seen an NFC sticker, you've likely unknowingly thrown them away like you do before washing or wearing any of your newly purchased clothing.

As with QR Codes, NFC can be used to set up a scavenger hunt or for any number of other fun activities for children or adults.

But, there are several varieties. For example, there are plain round stickers that work on a metal surface; small thumbnail sized stickers, white, clear or color, and probably many more varieties on the drawing board. You can look them up - they're sold on Amazon.com.

They're used on:
- I.D. Cards
- Consumer electronics
- E-tickets
- For employee or other access
- Loyalty Cards
- And more . . .

The Difference between QR Codes and NFC

NFC Tags:

These are digital, enabled by radio frequency. They can be scanned from a short distance, not requiring good lighting or more than a couple of seconds for a successful scan. They're based on a universal NFC Tag Codec.

QR Codes:

QR Codes require software to be installed. You need to bring the QR Code scanner up before beginning the scan. Your smartphone needs to be equipped with a good camera, and it must be daylight or you must be in a well-lit area in order for them to work. They are not universally coded.

Some are saying, "The NFC Tag is what the QR Code should have been." They've been discussed online since at least 2012 so you can learn much more by doing a search.

Regardless of your preference between NFC Tags and QR Codes . . . they and other mobile marketing strategies are projected to skyrocket in the next three to five years. Is your business ready?

Almost every category of business can use Mobile Marketing, including handy tools like QR Codes and NFC tags to their advantage. It's limited only by your imagination and creativity. Your local Internet Marketing professional can help you strategize to achieve the most value from mobile.

Oh, and let's not forget iBeacons! You'll start seeing these inside retail stores, if you haven't already. They work by radio frequency and are attached to central locations within merchandise departments. They're a function of indoor location based marketing.

Apple uses them with Bluetooth technology and they're said to be tested in large stores in selected cities during the 2014 Christmas season.

They involve placing a small hardware device in key places within a retail establishment, much the same as with NFC tags.

Customers who have downloaded the store's app can be communicated with by text message and can receive a percentage off coupon or information about an item in the department that they're shopping in.

This is similar to "geo-fencing", another location based marketing strategy.

Without mobile technology and the huge popularity of smartphones, these technologies would probably not have been developed for use in the marketing industry.

In the next chapter, you'll learn about "Local Marketing", which is just as important on mobile as on a desktop computer. This is a "must-read"!

Local Marketing

What is Local Marketing?

The short answer is – it's about <u>getting found online</u>, regardless of whether the potential customer looking for what you sell is on a desktop, tablet, or smartphone. You probably agree that's pretty important, right?

You've no doubt done your share of online searching. Searching for a local business is a bit different from an ordinary search with the intent to find information about something that may come from anyplace in the world.

For example, information about "golf", "fishing", or "how to-do" most anything can be global. Local is, of course, very relevant to geographical location. The search query includes the desired location, in most cases.

The Origin of Local Marketing

Local Marketing was conceived of by Google as they noted the high percentage of search queries with geographic qualifiers, such as "Dentist, San Francisco, CA".

Google's standards are very high and their focus is to maintain their status as the most accurate and relevant search engine.

Their paid advertising (AdWords) is a huge part of their business and it relies on accuracy and relevancy. Their method for organizing locally by cataloging "every Place in the world" (think about a huge library system) consisted of **Google Places** when I was introduced to it.

On May 30, 2012, they introduced Google Plus, adding a social layer to Google Places. It became known as their Google Plus Local Pages. Within less than a year the entire world was migrated to that new platform.

I remember that date because I had submitted an article for a print magazine (Toastmaster Magazine), months before, and had recently learned that it had been accepted for publication in the July, 2012 issue.

It was all about how the local Toastmasters clubs could use Google Places - out-of-date when finally published! But, they did allow me to submit a short update for the following month.

Very frustrating, but these continuous changes are typical for digital marketing, and print magazines plan months ahead. If I had published this book earlier, this chapter would have been out-of-date because another update was made.

The Latest Update

The great news about this latest version is that, though I told you earlier this book would provide just the "what" and the "why" of digital marketing, there's no reason you can't get set up with your Local Marketing by yourself.

It will help you tremendously and Google has really simplified the process with this update.

If you're in a very competitive environment, you'll probably need to get help from your Local Internet Marketer in order to rank above the competition, but it will still be well worth your while to follow the prompts and perform the basic functions.

Get started by going to Google. You'll need to sign in there first. It's easy to set up an account if you don't already have one. You can manage any of their properties for your business, such as Blogger, You Tube, and others using this login.

If you think you may want to assign the management of this function to an expert or an employee, you should set up a Google account with an email address that is different than the one you use for your personal communications.

If you do this, it's probably a good idea to create a an email account using Gmail, as this could be required by Google at some point in the future. They like for people to use their online properties.

Once you've signed in, your choice will be "Google My Business", which is what it's now known as. It's at http://google.com/business. Once you're signed in, you'll see the options.

Much of this platform is quite similar to Facebook. A person needs to have an individual Google + account to manage a Page. A Page can be set up for a Storefront, Service Area (great if you operate a business from your home) or a Brand.

The service area is applicable only if you **go to clients to perform a service**, rather than having them come to you. It allows you to hide your home address and designate a service area for a certain number of miles from your home.

The dashboard you'll be working from now combines Google Maps, Places, YouTube, Google's local Adwords platform, and analytics details.

If you already had a Page, don't worry, your data has been saved and is still there. If you have a website, Google will have aggregated information from it already, even if you weren't aware of that.

Once all your data has been submitted you'll be able to get 'verified', which will earn you a check mark on the banner of your Page signifying your verified status!

You'll then be able to begin implementing this powerful platform.

Besides Google, the two other major search engines also play a very important role in your Local Marketing strategy. Both Bing and Yahoo have a Page you can fill out with your business name, address and phone number.

Other web properties are important to "claim", too. Often a local directory will already have your business entered, but that doesn't mean you don't need to do anything!

It's very important that you go through any directories that list your business already and click on links that say "claim this listing", or words to that effect. If there is incorrect information, look for a way to sign in so you make edits.

Why is it so Necessary and Important to Claim These Listings?

1. Occasionally, a business may already have more than one listing. Of course just the one correct one should be retained. Google aggregates information to a Page based upon what they find online. If a business has moved, there will often be a Page with its former address, too. This is very confusing for consumers. An incorrect listing can be deleted, but you need to be signed in to Google first and must be the owner or represent the business owner. Again, there are verification processes to prevent unauthorized people from altering your data.

2. Throughout the Internet, your business data should match. Especially your NAP (Name, Address, and Phone number). A business may move, and phone numbers sometimes change, so regular updates are required. All abbreviations and spellings need to match, as well, such as "Street" vs. "St.", etc.

3. Photos, videos and more information beyond what Google has aggregated from other online sources and placed on your Page are needed in order to be competitive for search ranking.

4. A cover photo at the top of your listing, other than the default map will do a lot

toward helping your business stand out. Dittos for the profile photo.

5. You need to ensure that your listed <u>office hours are correct</u> – people on-the-go pay close attention to this. Google has in the past given precedence to businesses of a specific category according to whether it is open or closed at the time of the prospective customer conducts the search.

Local listings, such as Yelp, Kudzu, Insider Pages, Hot Frog, Yellow Pages and such are known as "Citations" in the Local Internet Marketing world. A citation consists of your NAP (Name, Address and Phone Number).

To find all relevant local listings websites, use Google to search "Local Business Listings, your city and state". There are some geographical variations beyond about the top fifteen or so.

If you're a professional, check out all the industry listings relevant to your profession to be sure you are listed there. Also, do read the chapter on Content, and especially the one that follows it on "Authority Marketing". These are higher end services, not as simple as filling in your profile, but they can result in growing your practice with clients, patients, or customers you enjoy serving!

Of all the pillars of local business marketing mentioned, Local Marketing seems most often ignored. Even though it's vitally important, and it's free, so far, anyway.

So the only reason it's being ignored must be that business owners are unaware of its importance (or, existence). But, YOU now know! Implementation is the key to success. Hurry! Before your most aggressive competitor beats you to it! ☺

Since it isn't apparent how many prospective clients **don't visit a business** (or fill in the "place") because it's invisible on a local search, this is the most common example of **Laggards Tax™** being levied!

What is the result when you search for your category of business and its location?

If you've never tested this, now is as good a time as any. If you enter your primary business category and location and your business doesn't appear, this will indicate the level of importance local marketing represents!

If you find you're invisible to prospective customers, you'll definitely want to act quickly in getting your SEO and Local Marketing up to speed.

If a skilled SEO specialist is taking care of your site (hopefully), adding new keywords over time, and staying cutting edge on Google algorithms, you will rank very highly compared to your local competitors.

And, this specialist can interpret analytics reports and keep you informed on your web presence performance and how it compares to your competitors. This means you can accurately measure your return on investment and make tweaks to improve it.

Analytics should not be ignored, as they're the only scientific measure of online progress and success. Having a centralized dashboard for this task is a huge improvement. Internet marketers watch their numbers like a hawk and do testing and frequent tweaking on a daily basis.

Be aware of the fact that geographic location is part of the equation when searching. You've no doubt seen and responded to the pop-up message, "Do you want to use your current location?" on your smartphone.

When you click 'Yes', the nearest business of your specified category will generally appear ahead of those further away, other factors and algorithm-changes-in progress notwithstanding.

Of course, if you enter the website name of your business, it will always come up, unless your hosting company has a server down or something. This has nothing to do with an indication of ranking in comparison to competitors.

Results will vary between a search query of your business <u>category</u>, the <u>name of your website/business</u> and <u>your name</u>. If you're a professional; a real estate agent, doctor, dentist, accountant, or attorney, search for your name.

If you find very little, you may want to act on the information in the Content and Authority Marketing chapters later in this book. Nick Nanton said it well, (paraphrasing) 'people may think you're in the FBI's undercover program' if your name doesn't come up online.

You'll definitely want greater visibility, preferably Press Releases as well as interesting and informative articles, or videos written or produced by (or for) you. Contributing to professional journals or relevant organization articles is great, too.

Research (Forrester, Nielson, ComScore and other researchers release periodic study results) has shown that local consumers search first for the category of business and location, "Los Angeles, CA, Attorney", for example. Then, when they're trying to make a decision between two or three, they'll often look up the owner or professional's name.

From the perspective of potential clients, being able to bring up information about you that is related to your business is reassuring. Before calling a professional, people like to see a photo of you and learn a bit about your accomplishments, special interests, and hobbies.

It means a lot to them when they find something in common they can relate to.

Discovering that you are the local authority in your industry works well to tip the scales in your favor, too. Seeing that you've written a book on your business niche goes a long way toward creating trust in your competence.

A Great Online Presence Requires a Persistent Effort

Many local business owners haven't recognized this, but really, marketing your business online is a continuous **recurring process**. There are four primary reasons for this:

1. **Change** – the one consistency in internet marketing. It's not just Google, but every existing platform and the addition of new ones, as well.

2. **Your competitors**. It's doubtful they share their marketing plans with you. They may sign an exclusive contract with

a Local Internet Marketer or unbeknownst to you contract with an SEO (Search Engine Optimization) specialist or Celebrity Marketer. Either way, you could unexpectedly get buried in the ranking competition. Exclusive contracts are common and require that the marketer providing the services refrain from taking on a similar client within a set number of miles. Their exclusive client will have every advantage. Of course, that exclusive client **could be you**, should you choose to make that request.

3. **The need for fresh content.** The next chapter is all about Content Marketing. From an SEM (Search Engine Marketing) standpoint it's about having articles, press releases, blog posts and social media posts, geographically optimized images, videos, infographics, and more . . . using the best 'keywords' for your industry – in the right proportion.
4. **The need to be optimized for additional Keywords.** If you own a restaurant, you'll want to show up on search engines for as many of your types of menu choices as possible. This takes time to accomplish, so while also monitoring all of the above, most SEO specialists monitor the latest keyword stats, and then add to your ability to be

found for even more of those keywords each month.

5. **Recurring Competitive Analysis.** You don't have time to keep tabs on what your competitors are up to. That's why your SEO specialist handles that for you. They do a periodic assessment; send you the analytics, as well as information about what actions they are taking to keep your business ahead of the pack. You should take the time to review these stats and ask any questions you have. These important services are normally contracted over a specific time and your business will benefit by continuing long-term with a maintenance plan.

The next chapter covers Content Marketing.

Content Marketing

Stale, dry never changing 'profiles' can bring on a yawning session pretty quickly, so it's good to make sure there's some fresh lively news about your business sprinkled in with all those important, but ho hum "Citations" mentioned in the "Local Marketing" chapter.

Your business isn't boring, is it?

Of course not! Well, it doesn't have to look that way online, either!

What is Content Marketing?

Content marketing encompasses a wide variety of internet platforms, as well as offline traditional methods of communicating with potential clients, customers or patients.

Content has always been important – the saying "Content is King" was popular back as far as 2005, and probably long before that. What does that mean?

It means that businesses need to have an ever growing inventory of information available for consumers to read, learn from, and enjoy. Through doing so, they will hopefully feel they know, like and trust the owner and staff of that business.

Research has shown that it takes seven or more interactions with a business for a consumer to eventually become a customer. Copywriters often compare this process with dating, then eventually falling in love and getting married. Email marketing plays a key part of this process.

Another reason content is king is simply that the internet is becoming increasingly crowded and that creates more and more competition. It's a challenge to create content that engages, inspires, educates or entertains as much, or preferably more than the competition.

Content marketing is a whole new focus within the marketing industry. It is merging with SEO more and more because it is after all, rather highly populated by keywords. And, there's another reason it's become so important over the past few years.

Algorithm Updates Have 'Encouraged' the Creation and Use of High Quality Content

Google Algorithm changes, such as Panda and Penguin updates have had a big effect on the trend toward creating quality content.

These algorithm changes come about unannounced and have relegated many marketers from super successful to the bottom of the barrel in a flash.

To be fair, that was often due to their use of "Black Hat" (against Google's 'rules') SEO best practices, though. Strictly 'legal' practices are referred to as "White Hat", by the way.

If you want steady growth without worrying about being caught and suffering for it, white hat is definitely the superior route . . . just like in every other area of life. Remember the 'Tortoise and the Hare'?

Google loves unique high quality content and rewards the creator with an edge in search engine rankings, though many other qualities (such as described in the Local Marketing chapter) are factored in.

Content Farms

Content is needed so badly by companies aware of that need that there are actually "Content Farms" selling articles on every imaginable business niche.

Thousands of writers toil over unique researched articles – and website owners and other businesses purchase those articles from the 'farm's' owner. This content is expected to be "evergreen", to be relevant for long periods of time. Local businesses need content on an ongoing basis, too, though few of them recognize it yet – but you now do!

In order to meet your content needs, rather than purchase it from these 'farms' you may consider hiring someone in your community to provide a steady inventory of written content. It will allow them to be fairly compensated for their work; while saving you money – it's costly to purchase from these 'farms'. And, "Shopping Local" is good!

Many older and disabled people have excellent writing skills and a desire to earn additional income. 'Back in the day' students became very adept at English and spelling! Not to mention, good old-fashioned work ethics.

Forms of Content

"Content" can be in the form of text, image, video, infographic, meme, or audio file. Anything you can think of that can be read, viewed, interpreted via the human senses – and, of course by search engine robots!

It's good to offer content to accommodate people who like to read, others who would rather listen, and those who are more receptive to animation. Repurposing a pdf into a video, audio, or even a book saves a great deal of time and effort.

The need for a high search engine ranking where competition is fierce fuels never ending need for content.

Content is all the better if it has emotional appeal! Content is interesting, therefore, people like consuming it.

Especially stories . . . babies, pets, human interest stories, your business story . . . top the popularity charts. Sharing on social media and by other means is the preferred outcome. Going "viral" is highly desired.

Stories that tell your business story, trigger strong emotions, and provide insight about your company culture and values is important to help the reader know, like, and eventually trust you to the point of becoming a loyal long term customer.

Other stories illustrate a point, persuade and offer proof in the form of a case study, educate and inform, or simply entertain.

'Content' appears everywhere online (and off, too). Here are a few applications:

- Articles
- Blog Posts
- Websites
- Ebooks
- Direct Mail sales letters, post cards
- Videos
- Emails
- Newsletters
- All Social Sites (mini-blogging)
- News Sites
- Cartoons
- Direct Mail
- Text Ads, Mobile Ads, or graphic ads created to grab the attention of viewers and encourage them to visit a website

Well, you get the picture. Marketing requires the use of content, and always has. It's the internet that has opened up infinite opportunities to disseminate that content . . . throughout the world if you wish.

Opportunity is <u>Now Here</u> (Rather than 'No-Where'!)

Anyone now has the opportunity to hone in on their special talents and knowledge, test the ability to monetize that niche in the marketplace, then carry out their plan of action and accomplish great things for themselves by educating and helping others **through "Information Marketing" or consulting.**

These last two forms of "Mass Media" (the Internet and Mobile) have contributed to many people being able to achieve an alternative form of living – no longer confined to only the choices near home.

Local brick and mortar business owners have the opportunity to play in this massive playground of ideas and information as a means of producing additional income, if they choose.

Local business owners can benefit in several ways by ramping up their creation of content and selling information products related to their industry and area of specialty.

Or, they can offer complimentary reports to motivate interested prospects to provide their name and email address in exchange for that free gift. You'll hear more about lead generation and email marketing in a separate chapter.

In the Authority Marketing chapter coming up you'll learn why becoming an author is such a huge advantage to business owners, too.

A Content Marketing Specialist

I've chosen to specialize in Content Marketing because I've always enjoyed writing, I can capitalize on my writing experience and apply those skills to today's content marketing strategies and best practices.

My ghostwriting background ties in with what you'll learn about in the next chapter. I love that I can have a conversation with someone, and then produce books, letters, etc. that sound, even to them, as though they actually produced that content themselves!

It's fun for me, it saves them time, and gives them the freedom to claim authorship (after I've been compensated for doing the work, of course!).

Whether its copywriting, web content, advertising content, a book or business letter, it falls into the category of ghostwriting. It needs to be in the voice and point of view of the person or business it represents. It's kind of like acting, in that way.

Content Strategy and Consulting

Content marketing, like most other marketing and business projects needs to be planned. A yearly marketing calendar is ideal for this purpose.

Putting the necessary thought and organization into it helps to produce a strategy that delivers the expected and desired outcome. Once proven to convert, it can be modelled in future years.

A business owner needs to be actively involved in order to achieve a great content strategy. But you don't always have to do it alone. Staff members, mentors, and partners (sometimes loyal clients are great sources for ideas, too) may find brainstorming content ideas fun and interesting. It does take disciplined action to stay on schedule, though.

Many small local business owners don't have a clarified vision for their business, which is always helpful in planning content creation – clarity often comes through talking over goals and needs with someone else, whether a marketing consultant or a good friend.

Analyzing Content Marketing Success or Failure

Digital gives us the ability to accurately measure the results of many marketing efforts. Never, before the internet, have we been able to quickly tweak a campaign, immediately replace a poorly performing ad with another, or increase exposure of a promising ad within minutes!

Compared with "older" newspaper ads, this is nothing short of miraculous. It's certainly a boon to business, making marketing a long-term investment rather than a dreaded expense. Certain content becomes a business asset to be re-purposed or re-used as a proven profit generator repeatedly.

We have so much information available to us today. We can select demographics and drill down to find and communicate with our ideal clients.

This allows for targeting only clients you want to serve, versus the "shot-in-the-dark" methods of prior years before technology made measurement of results more viable. Continuous testing for what works best is the norm today.

Savvy small business owners will want to be avid practitioners of content marketing, as they'll see the potential for unbelievable success.

"Publish or Perish" is an expression used by top marketers (I believe Dan Kennedy used this in a recent book, but am not certain) to signify the importance of content to the growth of every local business.

Authority (Celebrity) Marketing

According to Dan Kennedy, generally and deservedly considered the most famous Direct Response Marketing professional of our time, we each have a responsibility to manage and continually monitor our identities and reputations.

His outstanding results demonstrate the power and precise effect of such efforts. The opportunity for everyone to follow his lead is available to all in this exciting era we live in . . . and doing so for the purpose of business growth is the topic of this chapter.

After reading the preceding paragraph, did you think, "well, who is this Dan Kennedy, anyway, I've never even heard of him! So, what do you mean, he can't be a celebrity - since I haven't heard of him!"

You're absolutely right! He's not a celebrity **in the sense that Hollywood stars and starlets are**.

But, mention his name to anyone who has entered the internet marketing space as a serious student, or to marketing executives of the many large and small corporations who've hired him for his effective top level Copywriting and marketing skills and they <u>DO KNOW and respect Dan Kennedy</u>.

This should put your mind at ease if the very thought of becoming a celebrity feels threatening in any way. Celebrity Marketing means you'll become well known **to your target market**. So, don't worry about needing to learn how to fight off the paparazzi! And, don't expect any to pursue you.

Instead, think about growing your business by attracting new customers – that's all.

And, please, work on your natural reluctance to use Authority Marketing FIRST – before your local competitors! It's okay to lead!

Unless you're a "beta-tester" I've given this book to, the fact that you're reading this is likely an indication that you're considering the possibility of "upping your game". That's smart thinking, as we should all avoid 'playing small', even though that feels so comfortable and normal to many of us.

There is so much 'noise' out there, people are assaulted 24 x 7 x 365 with ads and they tend to tune out. This means we need to go the extra mile in order to stand out! This doesn't mean we need to do wild things like engineering wardrobe malfunctions revealing all, though.

Many local business owners don't consider the possibility - or the advantages of being featured in national media sources. They tend to dismiss the idea of gaining publicity, as though it's selfish and self-serving. I used to believe that, too, but not anymore.

Not that you won't be criticized, but this is where the "grow a [*really*] thick skin" advice is so appropriate! The more successful you become, the more you'll need it. The rewards are great though, so stay strong.

Many of us prefer to remain behind the scenes, but as a business owner you should consider being the face of your business.

Though you may be local and serve local clients, customers or patients, consumers do pay attention to media. Media coverage represents credibility and 'star' quality to them. So, all other things being equal, who are they most likely to call?

When they repeatedly see a name in various well known media sources over time, and read educational content attributed to that person they recognize that individual as someone of significance.

That person has been successfully positioned as an authority in his/her respective profession . . . quite intentionally, with the goal being business growth.

May I ask . . . why shouldn't that person be **YOU?**

An Authority Marketer makes it happen. A local Internet Marketer who specializes in Authority Marketing has received advanced training in that specialty.

It's somewhat new, and differs from the efforts a PR agent has traditionally employed, as it is enabled by technical innovations that certainly didn't exist until fairly recently.

Though Authority Marketing isn't for everyone, it is fast and effective for many professionals and for executives who wish to pursue new opportunities for professional growth – and a higher salary.

Those who help business owners with Authority Marketing select their clientele carefully from talented professionals who have proven qualifications, as well as responsible values and ethics.

With the inherent power in this <u>it would be irresponsible to promote someone who was actually incompetent or unethical</u>.

After all, we've seen unfortunate results of this in political races.

For years, many business success strategists have recommended that a person with expertise simply **call themselves an expert**. With Authority Marketing, **a third person is calling you the expert**. Psychologically, this is certainly much more powerful, and marketing principles are largely based upon psychological triggers.

Being interviewed is much more impressive than simply writing an article yourself, about you! It indicates that your high level of qualifications and performance level merit an interview from a journalist with multiple connections with the national media.

If you feel national news coverage, such as being quoted, featured or interviewed on major national news media networks could help your professional practice grow and help you serve a more ideal clientele, contact your Local Internet

Marketer or search online for an Authority marketing professional near you.

It's now well within the realm of possibility for a local business owner to be "quoted on CNN" "Featured in the Wall Street Journal", "Seen on ABC News!" or "interviewed on Fox News" and other major national media affiliates. This positions you with instant credibility and trust in the minds of most consumers.

Announcing this coverage in press releases, on your website, business cards, etc. provides that one last 'tipping point' when potential clients are choosing between just a couple of final runners-up.

This is an awesome side of content marketing, a perfect alignment of marketing principles with technical innovation and Public Relations performed according to long-adhered-to Best Practices.

It represents a very high perceived value in the minds of prospective clients, loan officers, and potential business partners, those who are likely to search for you by name, rather than for keywords describing what you do (both are valuable and necessary, as already mentioned).

The greatest advantage of the internet is that it has leveled the playing field as far as cost to entry. Yet, sadly, many people who really are ethical professionals whose work performance places them in expert status find it difficult to confidently claim the authority they truly rate.

A Priest and spiritual author, named Henri Nouwen, is quoted as having said, "The greatest trap in our life is not success, popularity or power, but self-rejection."

If you're anything like me, I'm sure you can identify with that statement. Being confident all the time (or even at all) isn't easy, but it is a goal well worth pursuing.

Most of us weren't raised to "toot our own horns" or to think too highly of ourselves; we were taught to have humility.

One point of view that woke me up, though, was 'hiding what we can do to help people is actually a selfish act'. I've heard it stated by several people, and I think it's difficult not to agree with. Being selfish is certainly something I don't want to be known for.

How about you? Are you hiding from the very people who may desperately need your help? Are you doing them a favor by remaining hidden? I would have to say "no". But, what do you think?

You may agree that unless a business owner makes every effort to spread the word about his/her capabilities to help target clients, no one is being helped, including the business owner.

Maybe you don't have any issues at all with creating a little fame to help your business grow. Congratulations, if that's the case! That means you have no obstacles . . . it's an advantageous position to begin with.

Regardless of which extreme you're coming from, the fact is anyone can pursue this. We can all challenge ourselves to do what's best for ourselves, our families, and our clients. Attracting the attention of prospective customers whose lives we can enrich fulfills this goal.

There's nothing more valuable to us and those who depend on us than our livelihood, so we need to preserve it.

Lack of confidence certainly does seem to run rampant, though. People tell me they don't really consider themselves an expert, sometimes after years of college and professional experience. And even after having earned a doctorate degree!

It's starting to look like an epidemic, this lack of confidence! But, I do understand, it took three years before I could bring myself to put my name online! But, necessity is great as a form of 'tough love' and change eventually becomes tolerable.

Every business needs exposure so they can serve as many clients as possible. We're all blessed with the advancement of technology that allows us to reach more people than ever before – at a lower cost than ever before.

The fact is **anyone** can now have their own radio show, their own television series, or special, documentary, webinars, infomercial and certainly their own book! Hopefully, <u>you have written a book</u>, since it's considered "the ultimate business card" . . . for good reason! Remember "Publish or Perish"?

You simply can't get a lot of information out about you or your business by uttering that 30 second elevator speech you hear about so much when networking is being discussed!

If you haven't yet invested the time or money into yourself and your business to implement this important task, I'd be happy to discuss that possibility with you. You and the future of your business will be well served by doing this!

This is a service I absolutely love helping people with. My "YOU-Nique Ultimate Business Card" book service takes care of the writing, publishing and marketing of your book. There is a qualification process – no doubt two-way, as a process like this requires mutually accepted participation levels and commitment.

Other than your taking the time to speak with me and read copy as I complete phases of the book, it's a done-for-you solution, and you'll get full credit and complete confidentiality.

If you don't care to allocate time for this, I can't help, though.

Since I do this writing myself, rather than outsourcing the work, I'm very confident in your receiving a high quality manuscript. It does limit my availability to just a few such projects per year, though. I'm not one of those "write a book in a weekend" proponents.

If that's what you want, you must eliminate me as an option. There are people in my industry that I respect highly, but I disagree strongly with them on some points that appear (to me) to support 'cutting corners'.

Things like publishing a book before thoroughly proofreading it, for example. I think it's a generational hang-up on my part - the way I was taught feels right.

I'll stick with the "make a good first impression" philosophy! Even though, I could be wrong.

You rate my very best efforts, and I guarantee you'll be pleased . . . unless we mutually decide we've made a mistake within the first one-third of the project and decide not to continue working together.

If that's the case, I'll return your deposit, but keep the rights to the already completed research. Sound fair? I want all my clients to be pleased . . . no, on second thought I love for them to be **ecstatic** about their book!

Here's how it works – we'll have our initial conversation where I'll have the privilege of interviewing you. From the transcript of that I write the first several chapters, I then submit the rough draft of that to you for feedback.

If you feel I'm on the right track with it, I'll bring the book to about 60% completion, and then you'll have an opportunity to review it again.

It's, therefore, a three-step and three-payment process. I'll work with you through up to three revisions in each stage to ensure you're happy and proud of **your book**! And, it will be yours!

One advantage of being quiet is that I can keep a confidence better than those who are super outgoing and may blurt out secrets unintentionally. No one will learn that you hired a ghostwriter – from me!

Your immediate reaction may be to dismiss this idea right away because you're thinking of the expense. But, then, you have to ask yourself whether avoiding the cost or adding the value is best. The cost is actually negligible compared to its potential impact on your career or business.

Many people have disciplined themselves and written their book over time by scheduling a specific number of hours each week, so that is definitely possible. It just depends on your situation, and it's certainly your decision to make.

Taking authority or celebrity a step further, it's definitely not unheard of to get articles published in national or global magazines or industry journals. You can become a weekly or monthly contributor on CNN for your industry . . . and many 'ordinary people' are also invited to be on local and even national TV shows.

These appearances result from consistent Celebrity Marketing efforts over time, and they will help your local practice grow! Or, if you want to apply these strategies for tourism purposes, to grow an organization, or to promote a product – it works well to accomplish those goals, too.

There is a Celebrity Marketing Agency in Florida that takes things to a really exciting level. It's very impressive. They host gala affairs for all their authors who've achieved Best Seller status. They have a TV show, and a number of other exciting events . . . with more being added all the time.

Through their work, they've changed the lives of thousands!

The next chapter will discuss Lead Generation and introduce you to some methods now possible that you probably haven't been made aware of yet.

Lead Generation

Seeking new leads is definitely not a novel business concept. It's a standard procedure for acquiring clients, patients and customers. For decades, people have been compiling and selling 'lists' to businesses. This is a topic every business owner is familiar with.

The reason it merits separate mention in this book is that new methods of acquiring leads have cropped up and hearing about them can deepen your understanding.

Before the Internet, most businesses had a 'Rolodex' with contact information for their customers, vendors, employees, and other business contacts.

Restaurants have collected business cards in a fish bowl for years, and most contractors ask for referrals from each customer as a matter of course.

The really important part, "follow-up", varies from one business to another. Some restaurants never get around to engaging with the owners of those business cards, some of which may have been there for eons. (The cards, not the people!).

Some stores never contact former customers about upcoming sales they might be interested in learning about. Some contractors forget to ask satisfied customers for a referral. And, some never get around to contacting any of the referrals they've received.

Without any follow-up, lead generation (Direct Response Marketing) obviously cannot be highly effective.

Historically, follow-up has been accomplished by telephone. Many people are uncomfortable with this – it often feels like that dreaded, almost-worse-than-death activity referred to as 'cold calling'.

The alternative, direct mail or post card marketing prior to the Internet was typically better tolerated, but could be a budget buster.

So, thank heavens there is this thing called the Internet . . . and let us not forget mobile, either! Email marketing has been popular in the Internet Marketing world since its inception. "The money is in the list" (or, more accurately, the communication level with the list as well as other factors) has been a continuing mantra. It applies to lists of mobile device users, too. And, it's been super effective. Some people have been lamenting the fate of email marketing, as, generally, open rates are down now.

It makes sense that a mobile list building effort might be more fruitful. Certainly, it is highly recommended, and you can either use text messaging or email.

It is so common for people to check their email on mobile, and they're also very open to reasonable use of permission based text messaging. People live 24 x 7 with their mobile devices within reach, so this has become more and more common.

It means that your list doesn't have to include only those customers who come in to your physical location. You can 'build a list' online. And, you can offer affiliate products that are complementary to your industry niche. This passive income source can defray a portion of digital marketing expense.

But, at the least having a "Landing Page" or Squeeze Page" on your website is a necessity. You can have more than one, too. This is considered absolutely essential for internet marketers.

Local businesses also benefit from the use of internet marketing practices, since consumers use the internet to find them.

Landing Pages include a brief sales message, a Call to Action (CTA), and a form visitors enter their name and email address into. With the internet and mobile, there are many opportunities for you to gather leads.

I'm going to stop here to share a lead generation method I've recently been introduced to. As of a few months ago I don't believe it had been offered outside the Local Internet Marketing community.

Social Wi-Fi Hotspots

This was introduced about a year ago and appears to be something that will be very effective for restaurants, nightclubs, casinos, resorts and outdoor concerts and such.

As you know, almost everyone has a smartphone or other mobile device and they always seem to be using it. Therefore, **they need a Wi-Fi connection!**

They're constantly checking their email, monitoring the weather or stock market, texting friends and relatives, playing games, listening to music, using 'utilities', and generally ignoring everything and everybody in their midst much more than they did in the pre-smartphone era, it seems.

So, what does this mean? Well, they're rather partial **to <u>free</u> Wi-Fi**! And now, businesses can attract them in by promoting this free service! It includes a built-in lead generation system for the business, too!

Cost effective, secure Wi-Fi service for customer use is now within the realm of affordability for any type of business. Or, for any event!

Make that "even more affordable" because Wi-Fi hotspots have just been integrated into at least one mobile marketing platform!

Along with NFC tags, iBeacons, and a host of other cutting edge features, some of which were discussed in the chapter on Mobile Marketing. This will become a robust platform, and other platforms will surely follow!

Your business can stay in touch with Wi-Fi users and keep them updated about your great deals and special offers!

You may want to ask your Local Internet Marketer about this, especially if you own a restaurant, casino, nightclub, or are a member of a civic group that plans community events.

This is, of course governed by the same rules against spam that have long been in place, and those rules need to be followed to the letter and respected. Again, we're only allowed to market to potential customers following their approval.

Getting Started with List Building

To get started, you'll want to sign up for an "auto-responder". It's basically a database management system that allows you to send messages to many people while only needing to write the message once (if you're using a mobile SMS platform, this is built-in to it, as well).

You've probably heard Constant Contact being advertised, and may already use it to some degree. It's an auto-responder, as is Aweber, Mail Chimp and a number of other options.

You'll likely be able to sign up for a limited time free trial. When the trial has ended these usually run about $15-$20 per month.

Autoresponders keep track of subscribers and give you information on open rates, clicks, and other actions taken.

Once you've collected a sizable list of names you'll probably want to begin dividing them into more narrow lists.

Adding CRM (Customer Relationship Management) software is a helpful addition to your ability to grow your client base.

For example members of your list can be divided according to common demographic differences like age, sex, education and income levels. Plus, it's important to understand where they are in the relationship with your business.

You do this so that the message each of them receives is personally relevant to them. Consumers dislike receiving messages about products or topics they have no interest in or that have no relevance to their lives.

So, after lists are created they are 'segmented' into categories. Surveys are often used to help with this. For example, a survey may be emailed out to everyone who joined a list marking them as someone interested in a broad niche, let's say Internet Marketing.

Everyone on that list may be sent a survey designed to place them in one of four specific narrower categories. To do so, the questions on that survey might ask, "How long have you been doing Internet Marketing?"

At the completion of the survey when most respondents have answered, that list will be segmented into people who have been doing Internet Marketing, let's say, "Less than nine months", then another list will include those whose answer was "More than two years, followed by a couple of other options.

Afterwards, each category become a separate list and the people on each of those lists will receive relevant emails appropriate to their indicated educational needs and entry date and progression through your "Marketing Funnel".

Don't worry, all of this information, as mentioned earlier, is just to make you a smart consumer!

Your Offline Marketing professional can help you with all of these details from setting up your auto-responder, preparing the follow-up messages, even writing a report or helping you decide on another free or low-cost item at the low end of your sales funnel to engage your visitors and motivate them to sign up to your list.

Clearly, lead generation is a vital step in growing your business. And, it plays an important role in the aforementioned "Exit Strategy", too.

Exit Strategy Options

No matter how much you love your business, you may sometimes wonder how everything might eventually come together so that you can retire at some point.

Some business owners pass their entire business down to a younger family member and that often works out well.

Others have no one set up to take over so they rely on selling their business. This can be a stressful prospect, as there are unpredictable considerations. Among your concerns may be questions about the net worth of your business at the time when you may wish to retire.

This is difficult to forecast due to changing economic conditions and other factors.

Your website could be monetized in a variety of ways that add information or products of interest to visitors.

Adding a FAQ (Frequently Asked Questions) page with answers to the ten or twenty questions people most often ask you about you're your industry or profession is always a good service to provide for interested visitors to your website.

This content could become the basis for your future book.

"Information Marketing" online is a huge business, and more and more local business owners are, reportedly, getting started with it. Two of my most popular ghostwriting projects are writing special reports and producing information products for clients to sell. I've done them on topics from candy, to backyard chickens, to eldercare, tax policy, medical, and many more.

This is only mentioned to demonstrate the possible upside for those local business owners who may look upon a website and other digital marketing as more of a bothersome expense rather than the valuable income multiplying asset it certainly can become. Consider the advantages to increasing your income!

This book isn't about 'making money online', or even Information Marketing, though. There are plenty of resources available elsewhere if this is something that attracts your interest.

For example, Dan Kennedy, mentioned earlier, works with a wide variety of small local businesses to help them gain additional income through producing and selling information products.

Some move on (or add as a sideline business) a consulting practice training others in their industry how to utilize direct response marketing or information marketing.

By now, most of the leading Internet Marketers have recognized the need for local businesses to gain a strong online presence and to take advantage of the opportunities available. Most have developed training programs or taken small local businesses on as clients.

Bionic Marketing

What follows is the story of how I ended up in the Local Internet Marketing business, and why I'm so excited and grateful for the technologies available to all of us today . . . in the health field, marketing, and most other industries, as well.

If you're anything like me, you probably agree that we're extremely blessed to be living in this exciting era of fast moving innovations.

It was medical technology that gave me a second chance to 'get a life', and I feel immense gratitude for that blessing! In fact, the difference between "then" and "now" is, frankly, nothing short of a miracle.

This chance was made possible by three complete joint replacements after a miserable couple of decades. Groundbreaking medications keep me stabilized.

Because of my 'new' joints, I've been called the "Bionic Marketer" by several people – I prefer to define it as having transformational strength, whether applied to one's body or **to the marketing of a business.**

At too young an age, I was diagnosed with Rheumatoid Arthritis. If you don't know, RA is a systemic disease that eats away at the joints.

At the time of my diagnosis there was no medication used to curb the inevitable destructive outcomes of RA, other than gold shots. They were ineffective for me.

For the previous eighteen years I had worked as a hairstylist, so the RA diagnosis changed everything in my life, including what I could do (and not do) to make a living. I had chosen my career at a young age, and never imagined anything would interfere with those plans.

A walk past a beauty college in Bellingham, Washington as a sixth grader had locked in that career choice. The school's basement windows were open on that balmy spring day years ago as I passed by with my parents on one of our weekly 'trips to town'.

The most exhilarating aroma was emanating from those open windows! To me, it seemed glamorous, and I knew I wanted to be a part of whatever was going on in there!

Later, I learned that it was the lovely aroma of thioglycolate made less revolting by the addition of a strong perfume of some sort. Yep, permanent waving solution! I know it sounds crazy; but in my defense . . . I was just eleven years old.

I remained irresistibly "hooked" on a career as a hair stylist, was awarded a scholarship upon graduation from high school . . . and the rest, as they say, is history.

For some strange reason I thought being a hair stylist would give me the means to travel. It didn't, but marrying a career Navy man did get me out of Washington state a few times and we've had several other trips together since.

After we were married, I independently pursued the study of Trichology (the science of hair) and nutritional supplements related to hair and skin health. Very fascinating.

When my husband was transferred to California from NAS Whidbey, I ended up teaching "Scientific Permanent Waving", which I had learned from Jheri Redding, at a high end salon in San Jose.

Fast forward many years . . . and back to Washington State. The more advanced the RA became, the more "unemployable" I became.

Nevertheless, I wanted to have a profession, or at least a job! So, every time I began to feel 'better', I'd start a job search. I love writing cover letters!

You may not have ever imagined a scenario quite like this, but I quickly learned that employers rarely hire someone once they've been forced to return to the interview room and help the applicant out of the chair – even if the interview had gone well.

I can't and don't blame those business owners though . . . in fact, I can laugh at myself now for my silliness and denial of reality. Don't worry, I'll forgive you if you're chuckling, too, as you imagine that scene.

My faith that I would eventually find that one thing I **could do,** and find the right clients who needed my skills never faltered. And it was actually my lack of success in 'getting a job' that turned me into a dedicated entrepreneur.

I knew my 'new profession' had to be something that would help people, but had no idea what it might be. Except, that I did feel an allegiance to my community . . . I've had help from many in the area, and I feel indebted.

Back when I could barely move, I insisted on being as independent as possible, but from time to time I'd get myself in a 'pickle'.

Sometimes it was a heavy door I wasn't strong enough to open; or being overwhelmed by the force of the wind on Whidbey Island.

I was so afraid of falling, I'd stop and tightly clutch the handle of my four-legged cane when caught in a windstorm - just petrified . . . my muscles were so weak during post surgery rehab. I knew if I fell I couldn't get up by myself - and that having others trying to help would cause excruciating pain.

An "angel" always materialized to help me – I got so used to it, I'd just say a little prayer whenever I got stuck and help would arrive within a reasonable time. I was very fortunate and remain full of gratitude for those kind and amazing people.

A combination of prayer and research brought forth my new career. It was June 14th, 2005. An online ad headline jumped out at me. It asked the question, "Can You Write a Simple Letter Like This?"

"YES!" I spoke back to my computer monitor, "I can do that!"

After all, I had performed admirably in what some called "Unmailable Class" years before (one typo was considered unworthy of mailing, and earned an automatic "F" – I never got an "F"). I began feeling fresh hope and confidence as I read that ad.

"Un-mailable" class was a Business Communications course, part of a community college small business accounting associates degree program I had completed as a first option for a new career after the RA diagnosis.

There are 10-key speed exams for accounting job applicants, and I was physically unable to pass them, so I wasn't qualified for the best jobs in that industry.

Back to that summer of 2005, I was buoyed by mounting excitement over that "Simple Letter Like This" ad, and began to enroll in a growing number of online courses . . . expanding from Copywriting, to Internet Marketing, then Local Internet Marketing, Mobile Marketing and more.

It was eye opening for me to discover Copywriting isn't about avoiding grammar mistakes or spelling correctly, though! That instructor who required exacting "mailability" would have a fit if she read many of the sales pages published online today! I can't help it; I also appreciate proper spelling and grammar.

Copywriting (selling through the use of carefully chosen words) is all about identifying your perfect client avatar. Then, picturing that specific person and writing to him/her alone. The writing is in the same style you'd expect if the two of you were sitting next to each other in a bar (a coffee shop works, too, thank goodness).

A great sales letter uses strong emotional and psychological triggers and alluring product benefit descriptions to 'attract' desire in the readers mind. It's a fun and challenging skill to study and master.

Copywriting, and Internet Marketing was a complete change and exciting career choice for me. My appetite for learning was never-ending. I was wary of learning any specific skill set from just one 'guru', though.

What if <u>that</u> person wasn't completely competent; how could I tell, unless I studied others, too?

So I did that. After all, there's plenty of mis-information floating around online and I didn't want to add to it through my own ignorance.

My goal was a clear and thorough "big picture" understanding of local business marketing, and I reached that point.

The confidence to believe you no longer belong in the student category doesn't come easily when enrolled in self-study. There hasn't been an affiliation with a college, no credits, prerequisites, or graduation ceremonies. The training was done primarily by working marketing professionals.

There's been nothing telling me that I've "made it", except for my own honest self-assessment. Those who teach sell courses; they don't get involved with measuring student progress or ensuring that students 'do their homework'.

It took a lot of work on my mindset in order to make the mental transition from "newbie" or student to serious business owner. But, I am there now, and <u>I am 100% confident in my ability **to help you!**</u>

My being bionic (turbo-charged with the addition of titanium!) is similar to your business being made stronger through leveraging the power of the latest digital marketing tools, properly applied and integrated with current strategies.

If you're ready to unleash the full power and strength of bionic marketing onto your business, the prognosis for the future health of your business is very bright!

Sure, there <u>are</u> downsides . . .

- Some of it is still fairly new - your peers may not be using it yet (will you wait and give them first dibs?) Or, <u>will **you**</u> lead?

- More new income generating strategies will be added that will need to be adopted
- There's a financial investment and a learning curve involved
- Some people in your life may advise you against it, saying "just wait and see", or "wait 'til the economy gets better".
- Persist, and your competitors may become angry at you because you're getting all the customers
- And, you might get so busy and make so much money that it will be hard to adjust to your new lifestyle

But at least no one will feel sorry for you because your business is weak and pathetic. Plus, it puts you in no danger, and involves no pain or suffering! I firmly believe it's the antidote to a sluggish economy for local businesses and their communities!

Conclusion

Congratulations on making it to the end of this book! This level of dedication shows that you're serious about getting more customers coming into your business so you can reap the benefits of higher profits.

Upgrading marketing to align with consumer habits and behavior can't help but accomplish that!

There have been a couple of critiques of this book – some believe I've shared too much information!

I'm not feeling remorse over it, though. After all, this book is an example of Content Marketing. And one of the goals of Content Marketing is to help the reader add to his/her knowledge base by sharing information of value.

According to Robert Rose of the Content Marketing Institute, "Traditional marketing and advertising is telling the world you're a rock star, Content Marketing is showing the world that you are one." I think he's a wise man.

Your clients will benefit from sharing your industry expertise with them, too. Here's how I see it . . . I am fully capable, as you no doubt are, of cooking myself a meal. If we agree on that point, shouldn't we question why restaurants are so crowded at meal times?

Even when a chef shares a signature recipe, customers often prefer to enjoy the restaurant's ambiance most of the time. Just because we teach our clients facts about our industry, doesn't mean they want to do the same work we do!

Besides, there is a saying among marketing professionals – it is, "**a confused mind never buys**". Since it is so vital for small local businesses to integrate digital into their marketing, my goal has been to alleviate any confusion and overwhelm you may have.

I hope I've done that for you, because fear of the unknown or confusion about how to get started often results in not taking any action at all – and action is rather necessary. **Nothing changes** without it.

To recap, just like you most likely do research to study the latest products available before engaging in a home remodeling project or buying a new car - you've learned an overview of each of what I've referred to as the 'four pillars' of digital marketing' and how each of those affect your business.

You are now in possession of solid information that can help you grow your business, even in an uncertain economy. Growth <u>was</u> **the outcome you envisioned back when you decided to 'risk it all' and celebrate your Grand Opening, wasn't it?**

I hope you're ready to exercise control over the one thing you still have control over in this highly regulated business climate. . . <u>that one thing is avoiding Laggards Tax!</u>

Thank you for reading this! Don't delay connecting the digital dots you may not have already known about. Start brainstorming and jotting down notes for your book (remember "Publish or Perish"?)! I'm here for you if you need my help with writing your "Ultimate Business Card".☺

info@whidbeymarketingmaven.com

Resources

Lately, I've read a few great books on business and entrepreneurship, as well as personal growth. I thought some might interest you, too:

80/20 Sales and Marketing , by Perry Marshall. Perry Marshall is most famous for his mastery of Google's Adwords platform. In this book he brings out the widespread accuracy of the 80/20 (Pareto Principle) into all of life. Find out more at www.perrymarshall.com.

No B.S. Guide to Marketing - The Ultimate No Holds Barred Kick Butt Take No Prisoners Direct Marketing For Non-Direct Marketing Businesses, by Dan S. Kennedy. Mentioned earlier, Dan Kennedy is considered the foremost Direct Response marketing leader! He has taught business owners in every industry over his long career and is also a very highly paid Copywriter. Highly recommended!

Influence, the Psychology of Persuasion, by Robert B. Cialdini, PH.D. This is fascinating. After reading it, you may want to keep it in mind, especially if you decide to shop for a new car. Available on Amazon.com

Pitch Anything, An Innovative Method for Presenting, Persuading, and Winning the Deal, by Oren Klaff. Mentioned earlier, this book draws upon recent brain studies and presents the author's sales methodology resulting from those research results combined with his past experience. This is an ideal book to read if you're curious about the part of our brain he calls the "crocodile" brain keeping us from wanting to explore new ideas and concepts. Check it out on Amazon.

Conversion by Frank Kern. I very much like and appreciate this book! This author is a legend in the Internet Marketing Industry, and for good reason. I appreciate his emphasis on great customer service and building goodwill. Strangely enough, he is the first person I've heard mention goodwill since studying accounting in college years ago.

The Charge, Activating the 10 Human Drives that Make You Feel Alive, by Brendon Burchard, author of several best sellers. Here is another author who has followed recent research on how our brains work. He's very motivating, an excellent speaker and trainer with content that will help any entrepreneur. It may give you some ideas about what may be possible for you after retiring from the "daily grind" of your local business. It's always nice to remain relevant! As some have said, 'retiring is like being put out to pasture'.

<u>Tribes-We Need You to Lead Us</u>, By Seth Godin. I've had this book for a couple of years, but it's one that bears re-reading from time to time. It's very thought provoking in its emphasis on our tendency to maintain the status quo, rather than adapt to changes around us. Seth Godin is the creator of the social site, Squidoo.

I recently read a book by Robin Callucci, who worked in the publishing industry for a number of years. The title is **<u>How to Write a Book That Sells You</u>**. You can look her up by name; I believe her website address is www.robincolluci.com.

<u>Step Into The Spotlight</u>, by Tsufit is a book written in 2008, before Authority Marketing, under that name, was conceived. It's a fun read and it explains why **"All business is show business"**. If you doubt whether you, as the owner of a small local business should take steps to create a public persona and generate more coverage online and in national media affiliates – get this book! It, too, is on Amazon.com.

<u>Story Selling</u>, by Nick Nanton and J.W. Dicks. I received this book very recently and stopped everything to dive into it. It brings out the need to use stories in our marketing and describes how the human brain works in reaction to stories. So much research has been conducted in the recent past, and marketing relies heavily on psychology. I highly recommend this book!

Launch, This book is authored by Jeff Walker. He is well known as the authority on launching products online. His book is available on Amazon.com.

Ogilvy on Advertising Copy by David Ogilvy, a Vintage Books publication. David Ogilvy was partner in what became one of the largest advertising agencies in the world. This book contains many of his ads, his commentary, as well as examples of ads created by other leading marketers of his time.

The Remembering Process, by Daniel Barrett and Dr. Joe Vitale. This is a very interesting book detailing the process by which we can
predict success at reaching goals through "remembering" how those successes occurred – before they happen. It's a new way to look at positive thinking, and achieving goals. It's available on Amazon.com.

The Motivation Manifesto, 9 Declarations to Claim Your Personal Power, by Brendon Burchard. What small business owner wouldn't appreciate being more motivated in order to accomplish more? This book is about living our lives with total freedom, more courage and independence! I already love this book, though I haven't had it long enough to finish reading it. Do look it up, it could be life changing for you! I'm sure it's on Amazon.com, you'll appreciate it.

*****

If you or someone you know is interested in learning more about Digital Marketing, I've listed the names of some of the people I've learned from over the past nine years.

Personal development (attitude and mindset) is an important element in surviving as an entrepreneur, and I've learned a great deal about that topic from many on the list, too.

The majority of people I've met or dealt with in this industry I've found to be hard working, driven to succeed, honest and honorable.

I'm appreciative to all who've played a part in my training program.

Yanik Silver	Jeff Walker
Russell Brunson	Steve Harrison
John Carlton	Seth Godin
Perry Marshall	Tony Laidig
Kate Buck,JR	Laura Betterly
Mike Cooch	Costas Peppas
Ryan Deiss	Perry Belcher
Michael Masterson	Dave Dee-GKIC
Michael Stelzner	Mary Ellen Tribby
Anik Singal	Mike Filsame
Andy Jenkins	Ray Edwards
Brendon Burchard	Bob Proctor
Brian Horn	Jack Mize
Dr. Joe Vitale	Joe Polish
Marlon Sanders	Dan Kennedy
Bob Bly	Jay Boyer
Nick Nanton	Brian Tracy
Clayton Makepeace	Kevin Wilke
Eban Pagan	Frank Kern
Wilson Mattos	Marci Shimoff
John Rhodes	Jason Fladlien
Kevin Zimmerman	Chad Pollit
Rich Schefren	James Wedmore

Terminology

Learning the 'jargon' of an industry leads to better understanding. Below are some words and acronyms that apply to both Local and Global Internet Marketing.

If you already understand them, please know that they are listed for readers who are less familiar with them than you are. If you're experienced, you may still find a nugget or two of value within.

Since you've probably handled the daily tasks of running a business for some time, you're certainly capable of understanding much of this topic, becoming familiar with the terminology will help. Time to implement it is most likely your biggest obstacle to doing so.

Above the Fold – The space visible on your computer monitor as you bring up a website, as in above the fold of a newspaper. This is where it's recommended that a website contain key information about a business. Phone, map location, what you do, for whom, etc.

Affiliate Marketing – Selling goods and services online produced by another company. Commissions earned vary

Organic – Gaining a good ranking on the search engines through proper usage of Search Engine Optimization (SEO). As opposed to 'Paid', Google Adwords, for example.

PPC – Pay per Click. Google Adwords falls into this category. You decide the amount you wish to spend per day, and then you pay a pre-determined amount each time your ad is clicked on. Facebook and other platforms also offer similar type ads.

CPM – Cost Per Thousand impressions (a single instance of an online advertisement being displayed).

URL – The location (address) of a web page on the Internet.

SEO – Search Engine Optimization – Choosing Keywords or Keyword Phrases that relate to your business. The act of ensuring that your website has a high ranking when these keywords or phrases are used as a search query.

R.O.I. – Return on Investment, used very widely, you no doubt already know this and keep track of it in minute detail.

B2B – Business to business, marketing from one business to another.

B2C – Business marketing to a consumer.

CTA – Call to Action. Example "Click on the button below to order", "Call NOW!"

CPA – Cost per Action. A method of online advertising where the advertiser pays for actual sales or registrations, rather than clicks only.

PPL – Pay per Lead – The advertiser pays based on leads the ad produced.

PPS – The advertiser pays based solely on sales closed.

CTR – Click through Rate. Part of digital analytics that represents the number of click-throughs per ad impressions, expressed as a percentage.

CPC – Cost per Click. The Cost the advertiser pays when someone clicks on a link.

Navigation – The process of moving from one page of a website to another.

SPAM – Inappropriate communication. An unwanted message of very low value.

Home Page – The first, or main page of a website.

Geo-targeting – A method of detecting a website visitor's location in order to serve location-based content or advertisements. Only those who have downloaded an app or otherwise given permission to receive messages will get them.

Inbound link – Comes from a different site to yours.

Outbound link – A link to a site from yours.

Keyword – A word used in performing a search. Or a word used in an invitation to join a mobile marketing campaign.

Keyword Marketing – Presenting your message to people who are searching, using particular keywords or keyword phrases.

Keyword Research – Searching for the keyword that will bring you the highest R.O.I. (Return on Investment). Necessary before beginning an Adwords campaign or for identifying the best keywords to attempt ranking for.

META Tags – Tags that describe various aspects of a webpage, such as Page Titles, image alt texts, etc.

Opt-in email – An email requested and supplied by your customer as a result of providing their name, email address, etc. through your autoresponder sign up form.

Autoresponder – A service that keeps track of data about subscribers to an email or mobile marketing campaign. Example – Constant Contact, Aweber, and others. Allows you to send to an unlimited number of subscribers while writing just one email per 'list'. Most marketers have at least several lists.

CRM – Customer Relationship Management. Software used that is very important for an online business for tracking individual customer demographics and history with your sales funnel.

Opt Out – The action a subscriber takes to remove him/herself from an email or mobile marketing list.

Permission Marketing – Gaining consent from your customer before sending him/her emails or mobile text messages.

Pop-up Ad – Messages that "Pop up" in a new browser window, on a website and other web properties.

Search Engine – A program (such as Google) that indexes documents and attempts to match relevant content to a search query. Google, Bing, Yahoo, You Tube, are primary.

Push Messaging – Sending messages to subscribers of a mobile app, messages are accessed within the app, as opposed to SMS messages sent through the standard mobile marketing process.

Remarketing or Retargeting – Ads that appear on your computer after you've visited a specific website. They follow you to every other site you visit! These can be annoying, especially when over-used but are reportedly unbelievably effective.

Bitcoin – A virtual currency used by over 600,000 businesses, including Overstock.com and other online businesses, as well as local businesses. Resides in a virtual wallet and is traded, both against other crypto currencies, and by itself - in addition to its use as a currency for purchasing goods and services.

Squeeze Page – A single page containing a strong headline followed by text or a video designed to encourage the viewer to leave their name and email address in an included form in return for a free or very low cost product of value. Also known as a **Landing Page**.

Email List – An online marketer's list of people's contact information, those who've signed up to their email or SMS texting list. "The money is in the list."

Marketing Funnel - This is very important in the internet marketing industry. Picture a funnel shape, with the narrow at the top. The first product or service is often free or very low cost. Other items are below it and in graduated price levels, from low cost to the most high-end offers.

About the Author

Vera Ambuehl helps local business owners achieve their business growth and income goals. She is sought out for her ability to recognize and zero in on her clients unique strengths – that even they are sometimes unaware of, then promote them.

She is considered a trusted advisor, educator and enthusiastic champion for the success of her clients and her community.

Through her advertising agency based on Whidbey Island, WA, Vera's clients have access to her highly specialized technical team for full service online marketing services.

Scott D. says, *"Vera has been ghostwriting and taking care of my website content for several* *years – its uncanny how she's able to sound just like me! She's ghostwritten several books and many articles for me, too. I couldn't be more pleased."*

Vera's "Power of the Pen" efforts have thwarted an office clique's attempts to end a promising employee's career; assisted resolution of a number of consumer abuse cases; achieved a positive outcome in a federal tax audit for a small struggling business; and facilitated positive outcomes from RFP's and bank loan applications.

Her custom resume and cover letter writing resulted in interview invitations for clients who previously had been ignored for years.

If you're seeking marketing consulting, business writing services, content creation or PR services email Vera at:
info@whidbeymarketingmaven.com.

Vera works with professionals who help their clients, patients or customers look, feel, or dress well – providing services that facilitate personal and professional growth through improved confidence - such as the following:

Salons/Spas/Boutiques	Cosmetic Surgeons
Cosmetic Dentists	Chiropractors
Holistic Healthcare	Weight-loss Clinics

Being an entrepreneur/business owner isn't an easy pursuit with guaranteed results . . . So, I thought you might like reading the following quotes (in case you need some encouragement or inspiration). Enjoy.

"Whatever the mind can conceive and believe, the mind can achieve." ~ *Napoleon Hill*

"To win without risk is to triumph without glory." ~ *Cornelius*

"Keep away from people who try to belittle your ambitions. Small people always do that, but the really great make you feel that you, too, can become great." ~ *Mark Twain*

"What is not started will never get finished."
~ Johann Wolfgang von Goethe

"Formal education will make you a living; self-education will make you a fortune." ~ Jim Rohn

"A leader is one who knows the way, goes the way, and shows the way." ~ John C. Marshall

"The price of success is hard work, dedication to the job at hand, and the determination that whether we win or lose, we have applied the best of ourselves to the task." ~ Vince Lombardi

"Success is working from failure to failure with no loss of enthusiasm."
~ Winston Churchill

"As long as you're going to be thinking anyway, think big." ~ Donald Trump

"Every time you state what you want or believe, you're the first to hear it. It's a message to both you and others about what you think is possible. Don't put a ceiling on yourself." ~ *Oprah Winfrey*

"Don't let your small business make you feel small." ~ *Brendon Burchard*

Or, stated another way . . . "If you think you're too small to make a difference . . . spend a night with a mosquito." ~ *African Proverb*

"I can do all things through Christ who strengthens me." ~ My favorite Bible verse

Thank you again for reading this!

Questions? Just email me, I'll be happy to answer.

Your feedback is welcome!

Website:
www.whidbeymarketingmaven.com

Email:
info@whidbeymarketingmaven.com

A quick word of thanks and heartfelt appreciation to my in-house IT specialist and husband, Carroll Ambuehl – who at the last minute saved me from needing to re-write this entire book! Without his "Magical Powers" for fixing hardware and software issues and for his love and support over the years, I would find life much more difficult.

www.ingramcontent.com/pod-product-compliance
Lightning Source LLC
Chambersburg PA
CBHW051705170526
45167CB00002B/541